BE YOUR BEST
LEADER
... AND BEYOND

Catherine Doherty and
John E. Thompson

Q-LEARNING

For UK orders: please contact Bookpoint Ltd, 130 Milton Park, Abingdon, Oxon OX14 4SB. Telephone: +44 (0) 1235 827720. Fax: +44 (0) 1235 400454. Lines are open 09.00–18.00, Monday to Saturday, with a 24-hour message answering service. You can also order through our website: www.madaboutbooks.com

British Library Cataloguing in Publication Data A catalogue record for this title is available from The British Library.

This edition, first published in UK 2003 by Hodder Headline Plc, 338 Euston Road, London NW1 3BH

Typeset by Servis Filmsetting Ltd, Manchester, England
Printed in Great Britain for Hodder & Stoughton Educational, a Division of Hodder Headline Ltd, 338 Euston Road, London NW1 3BH by Cox & Wyman Ltd, Reading, Berkshire.

Impression number   10 9 8 7 6 5 4 3 2 1
Year   2007 2006 2005 2004 2003

Contents

SERIES INTRODUCTION	ix
INTRODUCTION: LEADER	x
1 ANYBODY CAN BE, AND EVERYBODY IS, A LEADER	1
What is leadership?	2
How are you leading now?	3
Let the journey begin	4
2 SEVEN STYLES OF LEADING: FINDING YOURSELF	11
Your current leadership style	12
Leadership profiles of great leaders	18
Management by exception	25
Contingent reward	26
Management by objectives	27
Intellectual stimulation	27
Inspirational	29
Individual consideration	30
Charismatic – idealized influence	32

The nature of leadership 33
Which to choose 35
Others' views of your leadership style 39

3 THE WELL-FORMED OUTCOMES OF A LEADER 46
Effective leadership 47
Creating a well-formed outcome 51

4 THE BUILDING BLOCKS OF LEADERSHIP 60
What presupposes us to believe the techniques work? 61
The three-minute leadership seminar 66
Awareness for leadership 67
Rapport 72

5 THE BELIEFS OF A LEADER 80
Beliefs 81
Limiting beliefs 86
Levels of influence 91
Manage your state – manage your outcome 99
Dealing with internal conflict 105
Changing habitual reactions fast! 109

6 UNLOCKING PATTERNS OF COMMUNICATION   **114**

The leadership communication model   117
Deletion   120
Generalization   121
Distortion   123
How do you delete, generalize and distort?   124
The internal representation: the consequence of the deletions,
    distortions and generalizations   127
Self-talk   130
The leader's behaviour   131
Wisdom for leaders   134

7 UNLOCKING PATTERNS OF THINKING   **135**

Patterns of thinking   136
Big picture–Detail   139
Externally referenced and internally referenced   144
Options and procedures thinkers   148
Similarity and difference   151
Moving away from–Moving towards   155
More patterns   158
How can you change your pattern of thinking?   159

8 COMMUNICATING POWERFULLY — **162**

Using language — 163
Background to precision language — 165
How to use precision language — 167
Benefits of precision language — 176
'Fuzzy' language to create meaning — 179
Three words that stop — 187

9 INTERACTING AS A LEADER — **190**

Developing the role of leader – things that count — 191
Honing and improving relationships — 195
Feedback: opening the channels of communication — 196
Receiving feedback — 200
Feedback techniques — 202
What does your feedback say about yourself? — 206
The big and the little picture; getting them both right — 210
The gift of meeting criteria — 212
Collaborative outcomes – how to win at win–win — 216

10 BALANCING LEADERSHIP AND LIFE — **220**

The notion of balance for performance — 221
Creating balance through recognition of values — 225
Shiny sides and dull sides — 239

11 NOW GO AND BE YOUR BEST   **254**

Getting you ready   255
Fear from the past   256
Managing a phobia   261
Moving on – making choices   264
Time to choose   266
Go and do what you want to do   270

Acknowledgements

Thanks to our families, friends and colleagues for their support, patience and advice. Thanks too for all the clients we have seen make such remarkable journeys.

Series Introduction

Perhaps you have had an idea, or wanted to achieve something, but known that you not only need some skills but also help with taking the risk and doing it for real. Maybe you have thought 'it is easy for him/her but not for me . . .'

This series is written for people who haven't got the time (or money) to attend a long training course or who are not lucky enough to be managed and mentored by a star in the field in which they want to succeed. These books will be 'back pocket' resources that will inspire and give practical tips that you can read up on and use in the next few minutes. They will also help you feel confident in taking skills that you already have into new situations at work, home and the community.

Lesley Gosling
Q. Learning

Introduction: Leader

You **can** be the best leader you want to be. This book focuses on how you can become your best leader. The possibilities open to you are described through clear precise text and rich descriptions of how great leaders, international (and less famous), have made the difference that makes the difference in their leadership. The analysis of their actions provide the basis for over 30 exercises. When you complete the exercises you will have a remarkable and empowering insight into the skills of the successful leader and be prepared to make the difference yourself.

Each chapter covers a distinct area of leadership. Completion of the exercises in each chapter will give you an amazing range of new approaches to your leadership behaviours. In Chapter 1 you start with an exploration of how you wish to be viewed as a leader, and how you can create the future. Chapter 2 explores differing styles of leadership through the example of Sir Ernest Shackleton, the renowned Antarctic explorer who is acknowledged as a great leader in adversity. Christabel Pankhurst shows you in Chapter 3 how to create a compelling outcome for yourself that will inspire your leadership. Chapter 4 provides the building blocks of inspirational leadership. For those in a hurry the **three-minute** leadership model is included in this chapter!

Chapters 5 and 8 focus on the skills of a leader and show you how to build rapport, learn more effectively, gain insight into the minds of your followers, and communicate powerfully. You will learn how to be visible and approachable, and resourceful in a crisis. Chapters 9 and 10 turn the mirror back on yourself. You need to balance your work, lifestyle and check your beliefs and values are in line with your new choices in leadership you have developed in earlier chapters. You will check the shadows of success do not impinge on your changes – Chapter 11 gives you the skills to clear the way for going on and being your best.

The book will give you

- A good read
- A jolt to your thinking, and then –

The techniques for changing in the way you want to change.

Be your best leader . . . and beyond

John E. Thompson lectures in Leadership and Human Resource Development at the University of Ulster. John believes that personal choice and action is at the heart of leadership, and has developed innovative programmes to develop leaders using this approach. He utilizes Neurolinguistic Programming in his programme designs, and to develop his own skills has become a Master Practitioner and Certified Trainer. John facilitates experienced managers to learn and develop on Masters programmes in Business Improvement, Innovation Management and Cultural Management. John runs in-company leadership development programmes, has consulted with over 30 companies on strategic HRD issues and has been a senior manager in private and public sectors. He has published two texts on management development and 27 articles in academic journals. John has been an invited speaker at international conferences. His expertise was recognized by appointment as a non-executive board member of the National Board for Nursing in Northern Ireland. His current research publications indicate that the techniques of Neurolinguistic Programming in leadership bring significant change in leader effectiveness. John welcomes the opportunity to bring these techniques to a wider audience thorugh the publication of this imaginative and innovative series and recognizes that he would have been a better leader had he utilized these techniques in his own leadership in the past.

Catherine Doherty brings energy, innovation, flexible thinking and an ability to deliver the results that can make significant differences in people's performance. She specializes in working with individuals and groups, facilitating them to develop in a way that helps them to grow and develop personally while also contributing to the development of their organization.

Catherine's background is in Operational and Strategic Management and she has experience in working both in Australia and the UK. During this time she has experienced both the excitement and challenges of providing a service within financial constraints. For example, while working in a newly created Leisure Department in a London borough, Catherine was instrumental in setting up new systems and structures and recruiting a great team — only to have to dismantle it due to cuts two years later! Most recently, as Corporate Services Manager, Catherine managed a wide-ranging Leisure and Community Services Department.

Catherine is an NLP Master Practitioner, an ex-International Rhythmic Gymnast, Coach and Judge and now spends ridiculous hours trying to row in a veteran women's 8.

CHAPTER 1
Anybody Can Be, and Everybody Is, a Leader

Personally, I'm always ready to learn although I do not always like being taught.

WINSTON CHURCHILL

Leadership is something that can be learned by anyone, taught to everyone, denied to no-one.

BENNIS & NANUS, LEADERS – STRATEGIES FOR TAKING CHARGE

WHAT IS LEADERSHIP?

Wouldn't it be fantastic to be able to learn in a way that suits you and be able to apply that learning immediately, to practical benefit and to understand why what you then do enables you to lead with effectiveness and impact.

Leadership is not a thing. It is the ability to lead. The ability to generate ideas, communicate them and create the belief in followers that the idea or mission is worthwhile.

Leaders are all around us. Some have a title – Prime Minister, President, Chief Executive, Headmistress, Conductor, Captain, while others demonstrate leadership over a long period of time – matriarch, founder of the family business, political idealist, head of nursing. Some show leadership in the moment. For example, the nursery teacher who led her children to safety in the face of a knife attack, or the passenger in a capsizing ferry who convinced others to join him to create a human bridge over which many could scramble to a place of rescue.

The qualities that make followers want to support the leader are not the same in every circumstance. There is no secret list to be shared. The secrets to your potential are inside you. This book will tell you how to unlock your own ability to lead.

HOW ARE YOU LEADING NOW?

Are you leading in the way that you want to lead? If you keep leading in the way that you currently do you will keep arriving at the place that you currently arrive. This may or may not be where you want to be.

 None of us knows what the next change is going to be, what unexpected opportunities are just around the corner, waiting a few months or a few years to change all the tenor of our lives.

Kathleen Norris

This book will help you to aim for excellence in leadership and allow you to continue to achieve results in different circumstances. You will explore leadership with the help of some voices of remarkable leaders and voices of people who are just like us. You will learn techniques, hear stories and recognize styles of leadership that can give insight, confidence and new skills to enable you as a leader to be your best.

LET THE JOURNEY BEGIN

Nelson Mandela at his inauguration speech as President of South Africa in 1994 gives a moment of great inspiration by quoting the words of Marianne Williamson.

> Our deepest fear is not that we are inadequate. Our deepest fear is that we are powerful beyond measure.
>
> It is our light, not our darkness that frightens us.
>
> We ask ourselves, 'Who am I to be brilliant, gorgeous, talented and fabulous?' Actually, who are you not to be? You are a child of God. Your playing small doesn't serve the world.
>
> Nelson Mandela, quoting Marianne Williamson

Your first step to be the leader you want to be is to come on a journey into the future.

Where do you want to be as a leader? You can look into the future and make these choices. Imagine Ann, a leader who is saying goodbye to her team of the last ten years. You are a fly on the wall and you can hear all that people are saying about Ann as a leader.

'She was great but she never really achieved what she was capable of . . .'

'She did a great job and yet there was something more that I believed she could have done . . .'

'I have no idea if she believed in me and my abilities . . .'

'She once talked about her dream and then she got so busy doing things that I never really found out what that dream was . . . Maybe she can achieve it in her next job.'

'I liked her and yet I never felt I knew her.'

Ann, who is completing her leadership of this team, has not heard the words from others that she would like to have heard used to describe her as a leader and is disappointed. She would much rather have heard them saying things like:

'She allowed me to connect with her ideas and then really play my part in my way . . .'

'She inspired me to believe that I was capable of more than I realized and gave me the confidence to do that . . .'

5

'Her inspirational ideas and belief in the outcome she wanted to achieve were so compelling we all got behind her . . .'

'Change and new ideas never phased her . . . she always had a clear picture of what we could achieve . . .'

'She was great!'

Albert Einstein proposed, 'Imagination is more important than knowledge'. We can use this ability to imagine or foresee a situation before we commit others and ourselves to it.

You will already know of many leading sportsmen or women who use future thinking and visualization of what they want to achieve as a major part of their preparation. This technique is a powerful way to imagine your outcomes before you embark on them.

Progress now

Leave things as they are

Imagine that you change nothing about your current leadership and that this is your leaving party, and you are the fly on the wall. You will know how far into the future that this event will take place. What will people be saying about you? You may also want to listen to your own voice projecting its judgement on you too. As you listen to all these voices you may also be formalizing your excuses for not achieving your potential.

This part of the exercise can help you to realize that what you are doing now may or may not be getting the results that you want and if you had the opportunity in the future to re-run your past actions you could take some different steps.

Progress now

Create the future you want to see

Now go to that same point in the future. Imagine the experience and achievements you have had in between now and this future point have been fantastic. Everything has turned out well. What will people be saying about you and the way you led them? What will they say about your sense of purpose, the vision you projected for them to see? The beliefs that you held, and the skilful and capable way that you led them? What sort of environment did you create for them to succeed and at the same time be the best that they could be? This scenario is your dream come true.

As you harvest the comments you can hear being made from your fly on the wall perspective, you can also begin to imagine the steps you will need to take to achieve this wonderful experience – of people valuing you as a leader.

Make a note of those steps now.

_____

_____

_____

This book will show you how others have learned to become great leaders and teach you the techniques that will propel you forward.

Now that you know what the book holds for you, let's introduce you to Sir Ernest Shackleton, the Antarctic explorer, with whom we will explore different styles of leadership in Chapter 2.

Sir Ernest Shackleton is viewed as a great leader. Margot Morrell and Stephanie Capparell describe him in *Shackleton's Way* 'as the greatest leader on God's earth bar none' for saving the lives of 27 men stranded with him on an Antarctic ice floe for almost two years. Yet they pose the paradox that he failed to reach every goal he ever set. He failed to reach the South Pole in 1902 with Scott. In 1907 he turned back 97 miles from the Pole. On his expedition to the South Pole, in 1914, Shackleton and his men were wrecked when their ship was crushed by ice. Shackleton did not even reach Antarctica. Yet they survived despite being stranded 1200 miles from civilization and without communication.

They survived on penguins, seals and finally their husky dogs. When the ice began to break up, they moved camp, an 800-mile trip in rowboats. As some men were sick, they made a base camp and Shackleton and three others marched across the mountains of South Georgia, without any specialized climbing gear, to a whaling station. Two years after they set out Shackleton then returned to rescue those at base camp. Every man seemed in relatively good health, and in good spirits.

So, enjoy the discovery that this book holds. The discovery that lies within you. Just applying a few of the techniques and ideas within the book will stretch your mind, and your perceptions, and a mind once stretched never returns to its previous shape.

Further reading

Morrell, Margaret and Capparell, Stephanie 2001: *Shackleton's Way: Leadership lessons from the Great Antarctic Explorer.* Nicholas Brearley Publishing, London.

CHAPTER 2
Seven Styles of Leading: Finding Yourself

Ultimately, Shackleton is a success because, in him, we catch glimpses of who we want to be.

JONATHAN KARPOFF, UNIVERSITY OF WASHINGTON

Man is man because he is free to operate within the framework of his destiny. He is free to deliberate, to make decisions, and to choose between alternatives.

MARTIN LUTHER KING

YOUR CURRENT LEADERSHIP STYLE

Why do you need to explore your current understanding of your leadership style? Malcolm Knowles in his studies on adult learning has shown that adults must build on and shift their old patterns to absorb new understanding. You will know this is true when someone tells you how to do something you already know. Your reaction is likely to be 'why should I change – I already know this and I resent someone asking me to change my pattern!' So you may not change. You may not know that there are other ways. To change and learn you must explore your current view of leadership, compare your view to other views, and where there is a gap that you wish to fill, you will take action to learn. Your first step is to explore your current understanding.

Progress now

Leadership styles – self

This exercise allows you to identify your perception of the styles you use most and least. Listed below are some statements about leadership behaviour. Indicate how often you engage in the behaviours, using the scale below to respond to each statement. Please place a number from 0 to 4 in the space beside each question.

The numbers 0 to 4 represent the following ratings:

0 = never

1 = hardly ever

2 = sometimes

3 = fairly often

4 = frequently, if not always

1 _____I give a clear vision of what we need to accomplish.

2 _____I provide followers with a clear view of the goals we want to achieve.

3 _____I inspire others by focusing on the values and beliefs of the team.

4 _____ I put forward ideas that challenge my followers' ideas to provide them with the stimulation to change.

5 _____ I intervene only when there is a problem.

6 _____ I give my followers a reward when they succeed.

7 _____ I coach each follower to succeed.

8 _____ I change things only when they go wrong.

9 _____ I act as the 'motivator' for my team.

10 _____ I make it clear to my followers what they have to do to be rewarded.

11 _____ I mentor each follower.

12 _____ I allow my followers to decide how to reach their goals.

13 _____ I am viewed as someone who others wish to follow.

14 _____ I help my followers to look at their problems differently to provide resourceful choices.

15 _____ I provide my followers with the opportunity to do their best.

16 _____ I give rewards and promotions for excellent performance.

17 _____ I advise each follower.

18 _____ I make sure followers know when they have achieved their goals.

19 _____ I encourage rational problem solving.

20 _____ I believe I have gained the respect and trust of my followers.

21 _____ I make sure followers have evidence of goal achievement.

Scoring

Now transfer your response to the scoring sheet that has three questions for each of seven leadership styles, and total your results.

Total your results

Management by exception	Contingent reward
Q.5 _____	Q.6 _____
Q.8 _____	Q.10 _____
Q.18 _____	Q.16 _____
Total _____	*Total* _____

Management by objectives	Intellectual stimulation
Q.2 _____	Q.4 _____
Q.12 _____	Q.14 _____
Q.21 _____	Q.19 _____
Total _____	*Total* _____

Inspirational

Q.3 _____

Q.9 _____

Q.15 _____

Total _____

Charismatic – idealized influence

Q.1 _____

Q.13 _____

Q 20 _____

Total _____

Individualized consideration

Q.7 _____

Q.11 _____

Q.17 _____

Total _____

Plot your scores

You have a total between 0 and 12 for each of the leadership styles. Now transfer the scores above to the web below. Circle the numbers and join each of the circled numbers with a straight line. The centre is zero.

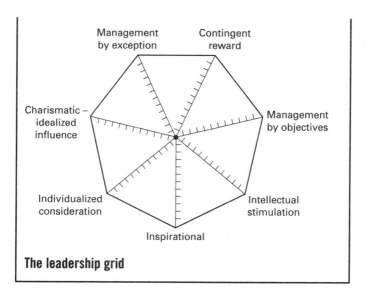

The leadership grid

What styles do you use?

You have identified your perception of your strength in each style.
A score of 12 means that on three behaviours that describe the
style you believe that you 'frequently if not always use that style'.
A score of 0 means that you believe you 'never' use that style.
Note your two preferred styles, and your two least preferred styles.

LEADERSHIP PROFILES OF GREAT LEADERS

You may wish to compare your leadership scores, from your self-perception, to those of great leaders. Bass and Avolio used a similar assessment on world class leaders using details from their biography. The scores are adjusted to fit with the 0 to 12 scoring scale used in this chapter. Only five of the seven styles are considered, Inspirational and Management by Objectives were not measured. It is interesting to consider the range of styles used and the impact that these leaders had and to compare your ratings against these.

	Charismatic	Individualized consideration	Intellectual stimulation	Contingent reward	Management by exception
Your score					
Martin Luther King	11.7	7.5	10.2	7.2	5.7
Mahatma Gandhi	11.4	4.9	10.5	6.3	4.5
John F. Kennedy	10.6	9.3	10.2	6.0	4.7
Abraham Lincoln	8.7	7.8	8.7	5.7	6.0
Adolf Hitler	10.2	3.0	6.0	5.7	6.3
Joseph Stalin	7.1	6.3	7.2	5.7	6.9

Progress now

To consolidate your views on your styles, read the descriptions
of each style below. The left-hand column describes what the
style is like; the right-hand column describes how leaders
behave within that style. Read each description and decide if
that is indeed your style. You may confirm your view by your
judgement on how often you use the phrase or words that go
with each style. This is an enjoyable exercise to reflect on how
your language reflects your leadership style.

What leaders do	How leaders speak and act
Management by exception Intervene only when the outcome will not be reached. Then give negative feedback and implement corrective action. Followers find acceptable behaviour by accident.	*Your behaviour:* Check if objectives have been reached. Take no action if everything is on course. See little need for praise or guidance. *You would say:* 'No news is good news.' 'I don't like that . . .'

What leaders do	How leaders speak and act
	'Are we reaching the objective?'

Contingent reward
Rewards are given that depend on (are contingent on) behaviours displayed by the followers.

Your behaviour:
Identify rewards for each follower.
Negotiate rewards for success.
Values incentive schemes.
You would say:
'If you do X, I'll give you Y.'
'So, no X, no reward.'
'What Y do you want for doing X?'

Management through objectives
Make sure followers have agreed outcomes. Encourage followers to use their own capabilities to reach the outcomes.

Your behaviour:
Work with followers to set objectives.
Set up systems to measure performance against target.
Discuss what people will achieve rather than how.
You would say:
'Is your objective SMART?'
'Have you met your target?'
'If we've stated it we'll do it'.

What leaders do	How leaders speak and act
Intellectual stimulation Use own ideas to compel followers to rethink their ideas. Emphasize rational problem solving and intelligent thinking.	*Your behaviour:* Challenge such thinking and stimulate alternative approaches. Value other ideas and want to know how they would work. Apply a rigorous analysis of the pros and cons of solutions. *You would say:* 'What problems do you see?' 'What ideas do you have for solving it?' 'How else might you do that?'
Inspirational Inspire followers through 'cheerleading'. Emphasize values and empower belief in future possibilities.	*Your behaviour:* Encourage followers' belief in their capabilities. Help followers to view themselves as high achievers. Get followers to focus on what they will achieve rather than what might hold them back. *You would say:* 'This is a great idea and I know we can do it.'

What leaders do	How leaders speak and act
	'There's nothing you can't achieve if you put your minds to it.' 'It will be wonderful when we do this.'
Individualized consideration The focus is on the individual's need rather than the group's. Individual followers are supported through coaching and mentoring.	*Your behaviour:* Stress the importance of the followers' values and feelings. Can easily see problems and opportunities from others' points of view. Readily put aside an idea and accept others' ideas. *You would say:* 'What is important to you about this?' 'Your views are really really important to me so we can succeed.' 'Let me consider this from your position . . .'

What leaders do	How leaders speak and act
Charismatic – idealized influence There is a clear mission and vision that provides a source of purpose for followers, a world is created to which followers want to belong. Followers trust and respect the leader and act towards the mission.	*Your behaviour:* When you present an idea, followers imagine themselves achieving it! Followers act without hesitation on your idea. Followers respect and trust your judgement and action. *You would say:* 'I've had an idea that we can carry out . . .' 'I have a dream for us.' 'I will never let you down.'

You will have had scores in more than one style. Consider whether your initial rankings remain the same as your understanding of the seven styles increases. As you read how Ernest Shackleton used these leadership styles in his Antarctic Expedition in 1914–16, notice how he used all the seven styles to different degrees at different times. This flexibility is something that made him exceptional.

Shackleton used *all* the seven styles in the survival of the 27 men in the *Endurance* expedition of 1914–16 in Antarctica.

The stages in the Expedition were:

December 1913: Announces expedition and begins to raise funds.

August 1914: *Endurance* leaves for Buenos Aires.

October 1914: *Endurance* leaves for Antarctica, stopping in whaling station in South Georgia.

January 1915: *Endurance* frozen in ice.

October 1915: *Endurance* crushed by ice and abandoned. Now living on moving ice floes.

April 1916: Set sail in three small boats.

Arrives in Elephant Island, 60 miles in seven days.

'Greatest boat journey ever' begins with five men – 17 days in storms.

May 1916: Arrive at South Georgia.

36-hour walk across uncharted mountains, South Georgia to whaling station.

August 1916:	Returns after four attempts to pick up men in South Georgia

ALL SURVIVE

Shackleton uses all seven styles *when needed*. If he was moving towards his outcome he would not unnecessarily intervene.

MANAGEMENT BY EXCEPTION

Shackleton felt confident in the ability of his followers to complete the task. He appointed a Captain, Frank Worsley, and left him to sail the *Endeavour* to Buenos Aires. He arrived in Buenos Aires and inspected the ship. He discovered the Captain did not exercise sufficient discipline with the men. They had given the Captain the silly nickname 'Weasel'. He told Captain Weasel he (Shackleton) would now be in charge. Shackleton found on his inspection that the cook was drunk. He was immediately paid off. Shackleton only dealt with those factors that were out of line. Shackleton did not make decisions without analysis. He spent several days checking what had happened on board before he went aboard as Captain.

CONTINGENT REWARD

Shackleton created rewards for appropriate behaviour. When he was fund raising for the expedition, he made it clear that the land would be named after sponsors. He asked, 'What shall we call it, this new land we have discovered?' His second-in-command, Wild, replied 'Archibald Dexter land', and 'Mount Jack Morgan'. Shackleton needed to secure the services of Hurley as photographer to the expedition. After telling Hurley strongly that he cannot give him his expected 25 per cent of the rights, Hurley prepared to leave the ship. Shackleton intercepted him, asked for Hurley's hand, and stated, 'Twenty-five per cent – wasn't it?' Hurley stayed. To secure the blessing of his wife, Emily, for his 'last' expedition, Shackleton proclaimed, 'One more trip south. That's all it will be . . . I'll be too old to go again after that anyway. I'll stay at home. I'll never take my slippers off. You can nail them to my feet. I promise.'

MANAGEMENT BY OBJECTIVES

Shackleton at times made sure that followers had agreed objectives although it is not a strongly used style. The only example is when he set goals for survival. His followers were prepared to haul the boats (20 feet cutters) over the ice, and all set goals together – Shackleton declared 'Robertson Island', the followers responded 'Robertson Island', Shackleton declared 'Five miles a day!' The men responded 'Five miles a day'.

INTELLECTUAL STIMULATION

Shackleton had an awkward follower in McNish, the ship's carpenter. McNish would often question the rational problem solving and intelligence of Shackleton's decisions. When Shackleton wanted McNish to make one of the cutters watertight he posed the question to him.

Shackleton: I suppose there's no way we can make the Caird [a cutter] more seaworthy without the wood?

McNish: Who says we don't have wood? What do you want to do?

Shackleton:	Make her unsinkable.
McNish:	Cover her over you mean? Make a deck?
Shackleton:	Yes, but I suppose that's impossible?
McNish:	Who's the carpenter around here – you or me?

And McNish did an incredible job with limited resources.

On another occasion Shackleton needed McNish to complete two tasks. He simply posed two problems. 'It's getting a little fresh up here [on deck]. Can you do something about it?' McNish responded, 'I can make a windbreak, sir'. Shackleton then posed the need, 'It may be helpful to have some way of visually signalling the helmsmen now we're at the ice.' McNish replied, 'Aye aye, sir'. Shackleton turned to Frank Wild, his second-in-command, and whispered 'As long as you never actually give him the solution.'

INSPIRATIONAL

The use of 'cheerleading' focuses on values and beliefs. When they are about to take the boats across the ice floes he quoted from Browning, 'For sudden the worst turn the best to the brave' – and asked, 'Let's make this our best shall we'. He inspired the belief that they all will be saved as he stated, 'My job now is to make sure you all live. Every single one of you. To do that I cannot afford to be sentimental. If I am, you will die. Die frozen, die starving, die mad. I've seen it all before. I do not intend to see it again.'

On another occasion Shackleton turned to them in a moment of crisis and told them, 'I can honestly say there is no finer group of men.' His speech to the complete crew as they left Buenos Aires for the voyage is truly inspirational.

We are learning now to carry on our white warfare. And our last message to our country is that we will do our best to make good. Though we shall be shut off from the outer world for many months our prayers and thoughts will be with our countrymen fighting at the front. We hope, in our

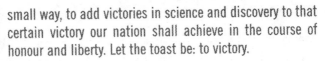

small way, to add victories in science and discovery to that certain victory our nation shall achieve in the course of honour and liberty. Let the toast be: to victory.

Dated Buenos Aires, 26 October 1914

INDIVIDUAL CONSIDERATION

Shackleton would take individuals aside, and coach and mentor them through issues that affected them. He joined Marston, an 18-year-old deckhand, on deck. Marston had fled the Christmas celebration with a note in hand. Shackleton asked, 'From your family?' Marston, upset, told Shackleton he was fine and to rejoin the others. Shackleton's subsequent responses were all aimed at building up Marston's confidence, and to move him back into the team:

Shackleton: I know, I'm fine too. I just needed a little air. Such a beautiful day. Do you notice anything?

Marston: What do you mean?

Shackleton:	Temperature's rising. We'll get there, you know.
Marston:	I know.
Shackleton:	Less than 500 miles. We're halfway. Skipper reckons we'll be inside the Antarctic Circle by tomorrow.
Marston:	I know.
Shackleton:	[holding up a cigar] You don't, by any chance, have a light do you?
Marston:	No.
Shackleton:	Well, come on then, let's go and find one.

And a revived Marston rejoins the group.

On another occasion he took Hurley, the photographer, aside to discuss why he had not chosen him to march across South Georgia to the whaling station. He informed Hurley that 'He'd like to have taken him, but it was right that you [Hurley] stay with the expedition. In some ways you are the expedition.'

CHARISMATIC – IDEALIZED INFLUENCE

When fund raising Shackleton created a mission and source of purpose for his followers when he asked potential funders to 'Close your eyes for a moment, please, and imagine Antarctica. Let your mind wander across a frozen sea, waves twisted into fantastical shapes. Icebergs like family castles shimmering in pearly shades of cobalt blue and rose. And silence. Utter. Absolute. Broken only by the thundercrack of splitting ice. The last page of that great atlas, drawn by explorers of the ancient world, lies open before us.'

And he then combines styles to use his Contingent Reward style as you have read. He asked, 'What shall we call it, this new land we have just discovered?'

THE NATURE OF LEADERSHIP

The seven leadership styles you have considered can be put into two categories, **transactional** and **transformational leadership**. You did not consider a third category, *Laissez-faire*, that is the 'do-nothing', 'leave well alone' approach – a non-leadership style. Indira Gandhi (1900–86), former prime minister of India, has been accused of being too laissez-faire in that she lacked the ability to react to avoid food crises and political instability. A critic said, 'My impression is that one of her favourite methods of dealing with issues has been to put them on the shelf and let them be forgotten for a while and let events find their own solution.'

Transactional leadership

■ If you scratch my back, I'll scratch yours.

Anon

The common elements in transactional leadership are that:

- The leader uses influence to encourage and support to develop a *relationship* with the followers
- The leader focuses on the outcomes and on the *tasks* that are the steps towards the outcomes.

Transactional leadership styles are management by exception and contingent reward. There are many transactional models that you may have encountered before. Examples are Hersey and Blanchard's Situational Leadership, and Blake and Mouton's Management Grid.

Transformational leadership

Leadership is creating a world to which other people want to belong.

Gilles Pajou

Transformational leaders have two common elements – the leader focuses attention on the *vision*, the image of the future outcomes attends to *actions*, the behaviours that move the leader and followers towards the outcomes.

The leader must attend to both. As Dilts points out, 'Vision without action is just a dream and action without vision is meaningless and boring'. Transformational styles include management by objectives, intellectual stimulation, inspirational, individual consideration and charismatic (idealized influence).

WHICH TO CHOOSE?

The transformational styles are generally seen as more powerful in any given context. The more 'vision' and relevant action followers perceive, the more likely they are to act in a manner that actively supports the outcome. When transactional methods are used, there is less impact. The view that transformational styles are more powerful than transactional styles misses a key point; you need to be **flexible** in your response to differing contexts. You need differing styles for different contexts, a viewpoint that is often lost in the fruitless search for the 'right' style. As a leader, all of the styles may be appropriate in differing contexts. Examples of response of differing styles by context are shown below:

Context	Leadership style
A team functions well. It typically produces good results and responds imaginatively and quickly to external change.	**Management by exception** Leave them alone: any intervention may stunt their creativity.

Context	Leadership style
There is a need to introduce a new production system over a week. The staff are unhappy about working over the weekend.	**Contingent reward** Offer: (a) triple time pay or (b) two days' leave for each day worked.
A new leader has taken charge of a leisure complex. There appears to be lots of activity with little direction.	**Management by objectives** Work with the staff to set well-formed outcomes for each programme in Wet, Dry and Personal Fitness areas. Once they agree the objectives, give them space to use their own skills and capabilities.
A new leader wishes to improve the performance of his school. He has a good young staff that is bright but they seem stuck and unable to come up with ideas and solutions.	**Intellectual stimulation** Set up and work with a focus group on key issues. Introduce creative brain-storming and analytical problem-solving techniques. Support them in their solutions.

Context	Leadership style
A product launch had just failed. The team had been previously very successful. They have just come up with what appears to be a great idea of the same standard of their many previous successes but they seem to lack confidence to make it work this time.	**Inspirational** Tell them how 'good' they are, how many successes they had in the past – and how wonderful it will be when the product is launched successfully.
A consulting organization has a very successful team that offers a well-branded standard training programme. One of the best trainers is to leave.	**Individualized consideration** Discuss with the trainer their concerns about the programme, see the issues from their position, find out what's important to them and be open to accepting their solution rather than your own.
Two different departments in the public sector have been required to merge. There is a need to create a new sense of identity to allow the two groups to come together.	**Charismatic idealized influence** You create a compelling vision of a world to which both groups want to belong. Present the vision consistently and with passion – and reassure them that they have your full support.

Different leadership styles are required at different times. Dilts advocates this approach in the utilization of the seven leadership styles:

The leader begins by presenting the **vision**, then moves to **individualized consideration** to connect to the belief and value of the followers; **inspiration** is the stage that connects beliefs and values to the vision. **Intellectual stimulation** helps the followers understand how the vision can be turned into reality, through action; **contingent rewards** and **management through objectives** provides the structure and system to maintain the effort and action towards the vision; if the effort and action are maintained through time, by the followers, the leader can move towards **management by exception** as the followers take responsibility for their own action.

OTHERS' VIEWS OF YOUR LEADERSHIP STYLE

On a leadership development seminar we ran, **Arthur**, a general manager, completed the self-assessment exercise in the following 'Progress now' box. The results confirmed his view that he had been using a style that was heavily dependent on intellectual stimulation and inspirational and management objectives to drive through change. He had moved away from using management by exception and contingency management.

Arthur decided to check his perceptions. He issued the Leadership Style – Others questionnaire to his staff and he received returns from 75 per cent. His results confirmed his perception. They perceived him as using his new found charismatic and individualized consideration styles, and not management by exception and contingent reward. He was pleased that his behaviour change had been noticed. There was an interesting sting in the tail to his results. When he discussed the results with the staff, they made it clear that they needed more from him in the styles of management by exception and contingent reward. He was perceived as not keeping his eyes on what was happening and not rewarding people. He realized that in his urge to develop new styles he had forgotten to use the other styles that his followers appreciated.

This final exercise is to score the questionnaire below which is worded for a 'follower' to score it for you. How you can use the 'follower' questionnaire is described by Arthur's experience in the case study on page 39.

If you wish to complete the questionnaire now rather than distribute it to others, complete it as if you are your follower. Stand in their shoes, see how you are from their perspective, hear how you sound to them and feel how you feel from their perspective. You can get an even greater sense of what they are sensing by adopting their body posture. (The ability to see things from different perspectives is further discussed in Chapter 6.)

Progress now

Leadership Style – Others

What is your current view of _____'s leadership style?

Listed below are some statements about leadership behaviour. Indicate how often _____ engages in the behaviours, using the scale below to respond to each statement. Please place a number from 0 to 4 in the space beside each question.

The numbers 0 to 4 represent the following scores:

0 = never

1 = hardly ever

2 = sometimes

3 = fairly often

4 = frequently, if not always

1 _____Gives a clear vision of what we need to accomplish.

2 _____Provides followers with a clear view of the goals we want to achieve.

3 _____Inspires others by focusing on the values and beliefs of the team.

4 _____Puts forward ideas that challenge his/her followers' ideas to provide them with the stimulation to change.

5 _____Intervenes only when there is a problem.

6 _____Gives his/her followers a reward when they succeed.

7 _____Coaches each follower to succeed.

8 _____Changes things only when they go wrong.

9 _____Acts as the 'motivator' for his/her team.

10 _____Makes it clear to his/her followers what they have to do to be rewarded.

11	____Mentors each follower.

11 ____Mentors each follower.

12 ____Allows his/her followers to decide how to reach their goals.

13 ____Is viewed as someone who others wish to follow.

14 ____Helps his/her followers to look at their problems differently to provide resourceful choices.

15 ____Provides his/her followers with the opportunity to do their best.

16 ____Gives rewards and promotions for excellent performance.

17 ____Advises each follower.

18 ____Makes sure followers know when they have achieved their goals.

19 ____Encourages rational problem solving.

20 ____Believes he/she has gained the respect and trust of his/her followers.

21 ____Makes sure followers have evidence of goal achievement.

Scoring

Now transfer your response to the scoring sheet that has three questions for each of seven leadership styles. These scores will give your impression of _____'s leadership style.

Total the results

Management by exception	Contingent reward
Q.5 _____	Q.6 _____
Q.8 _____	Q.10 _____
Q.18 _____	Q.16 _____
Total _____	*Total* _____

Management by objectives	Intellectual stimulation
Q.2 _____	Q.4 _____
Q.12 _____	Q.14 _____
Q.21 _____	Q.19 _____
Total _____	*Total* _____

Inspirational	Individualized consideration
Q.3 _____	Q.7 _____
Q.9 _____	Q.11 _____
Q.15 _____	Q.17 _____
Total _____	*Total* _____

Charismatic – idealized influence

Q.1 _____

Q.13 _____

Q 20 _____

Total _____

Plot the scores

You have a total between 0 and 12 for each of the leadership styles. Now transfer the scores above to the spider's web from the first exercise. As before circle the numbers and join each of the circled numbers with a straight line.

Final exercise

When the questionnaire from others is completed (or you have completed it as if you were them) compare your scores from your self perception to the perception of your followers. You will gain additional insight into the perception of your leadership style. There will be confirmation of existing style choice and also gaps in perception where you believe you rate highly and your followers disagree, and vice versa.

You now have a clear understanding of the 'What' of leadership – the seven styles. You now know what you can change to be an effective leader. The next chapter gives you the 'How' of leadership, based on modelling how successful leaders act. The leaders come from business, public service and the community.

At every level of an organization or group, and in every part of community, you can be a leader, if you choose to be one. If one can, anyone can.

Further reading

Bass, Professor Bernie and Avolio, Bruce: 'Biography and Assessment of Transformational Leadership at the World Class Level', *Journal of Management*, Vol. 13, 1 March 1987

Dilts, Robert B. 1996 *Visionary Leadership Skills: Creating a world to which people want to belong*. Meta Publications, Capitola, California

Morrell, Margaret and Capparell, Stephanie 2001 *Shackleton's Way: Leadership lessons from the Great Antarctic Explorer*. Nicholas Brearley Publishing, London.

Shackleton: a First Sight Film Production is available from the Channel 4 shop: www.Channel4.com.uk/shop, or 00 44 (0) 870 123 4344. The words of Shackleton are taken from the film.

CHAPTER 3
The Well-formed Outcomes of a Leader

If you dream it, you can do it.

WALT DISNEY

We are resolved that 1909 must and shall see
the political enfranchisement of British women.

CHRISTABEL PANKHURST

EFFECTIVE LEADERSHIP

Leaders who lead effectively do so by recognizing that their idea needs to be compelling to others. Those leaders with the strongest sense of their own compelling idea are best able to describe what the goal or outcome will be like. Done in simple ways the resultant well-formed outcome allows followers to align themselves and direct their own actions towards believing in and contributing to achieving the same outcome.

In this chapter you will:

- Follow how Christabel Pankhurst, as a leader of social change, might have created her well-formed outcome.
- Understand the technique for well-formed outcomes.
- Draft your well-formed outcome for a leadership challenge you face.

CHRISTABEL PANKHURST

Using the voice of **Christabel Pankhurst** we can analyse how a well-formed outcome is created.

Christabel Pankhurst (daughter of Emmeline Pankhurst) declared on 18 December 1908, a few hours after she was released from Holloway Prison following one of her spells of imprisonment there:

The militant suffragettes who form the Women's Social and Political Union are engaged in the attempt to win the parliamentary vote for the women of this country. Their claim is that those women who pay rates and taxes and fulfil the same qualification as men voters shall be placed upon the parliamentary register. The reasons why women should have the vote are obvious to every fair-minded person. The British constitution provides that taxation and representation shall go together, therefore women taxpayers are entitled to vote. Parliament deals with questions of vital interest to women, such as the education, housing and employment questions and upon such matters women wish to express their opinions at the ballot box. The honour and safety of the country are in the hands of parliament; therefore every patriotic and public-spirited woman wishes to take part in controlling the actions of our legislators. We are resolved that 1909 must and shall see the political enfranchisement of British women.

Christabel Pankhurst shows the elements of a compelling vision using a well-formed outcome in this speech.

To begin with, her stated outcome is described in the positive: 'women who pay rates and taxes and fulfil the same qualification as men voters shall be placed upon the parliamentary register'. This is because the brain has the ability to focus and create its own representations – the brain has the ability to fix on a desired outcome and create its own image. It is these internal representations in the brain that make an idea able to be grasped, and once grasped, committed to. Equally, the brain is able to fix on an undesired outcome with correspondingly negative results.

Other effective leaders also use visionary images:

 I see one nation, one people. Then I see us dealing with the economic situation.

Nelson Mandela, when in prison

And so, my fellow Americans: ask not what your country can do for you — ask what you can do for your country. My fellow citizens of the world: ask not what America will do for you, but what together we can do for the freedom of man.

John F. Kennedy. Inaugural address,
20 January 1961

I have a dream that one day this nation will rise up, live out the true meaning of its creed: we hold these truths to be self evident, that all men are created equal.

Reverend Martin Luther King.
Washington, 27 August 1963

We know how rough the road will be, how heavy here the load will be; we know about the barricades that wait along the track, but we have set our soul ahead upon a certain goal ahead and nothing left, from hell to sky shall ever turn us back.

Vince Lombardi, American football coach

CREATING A WELL-FORMED OUTCOME

State outcomes in the positive

Leaders who regularly achieve what they want are proactive or visionary in their thinking. They are firmly focused in the future, can describe their outcome and therefore are able to move towards the outcome and often achieve it.

Pankhurst's commitment to the future is evident in her words, 'We are resolved that 1909 must and shall see the political enfranchisement of British women.' She also uses compelling language to describe the outcome. Her vision is made richer by her references to 'women who pay rates and taxes', 'every fair-minded person', 'British constitution provides that taxation and representation shall go together', 'Parliament deals with questions of vital interest to women', and 'The honour and safety of the country'.

There is a clear technique for creating a well-formed outcome and we will now take you through the steps involved using the Christabel Pankhurst example.

Sensory specific

When you state what you will see, hear and feel in such a sensory specific way, you help to associate the listener (and yourself) with the experience and test for him or herself if it is something he or she wants to have for real. The more compelling the description, the more committed the listener will become. The listener visits the future you want to create.

Context

The context within the well-formed outcome technique is an important factor and is defined as when and where the outcome is to take place and who else will be there. Knowing and describing the context specifically makes the definition clearer. In this case Christabel Pankhurst is asking for votes for women who pay taxes as only men who paid taxes had the vote at that time. She is asking for the possible dream of suffrage on the same terms as men. Her vision is firmly set in the political and social context of 1908. She does not, at this stage, ask for universal suffrage, votes for all regardless of status.

Fit

How does Pankhurst's idea of women's suffrage fit with the rest of her life? We already know that she is willing to go to prison in pursuit of her outcome. Leadership of change does not come without its consequences. To understand what leading will do for you, it is necessary to understand what else will have to change in order to allow it to happen, what and who else will have to shift to fit in with the new reality that is envisaged and what physical resources are needed to achieve the outcome.

Leaders think about what holds back change. Christabel Pankhurst took a courageous stance, which involved her being imprisoned. What is it in the present that is resistant to change? If you can be stopped the goal is not yet well formed and may be unachievable. Work through the question 'What would it take to overcome this?'

The notion of secondary gain may explain why women before her were held back from taking actions such as Pankhurst's. Secondary gain is the benefit that inaction or current actions give you. If Christabel Pankhurst had not pursued suffrage for women she would have been able to live a privileged and settled lifestyle of the Edwardian lady.

Resources

Check whether you have the resources you can activate to get your outcome. For Christabel Pankhurst internal resources may have been what we would call courage and tenacity. External resources may have been funding and access to those with influence. She also had the belief that what she could do would have an effect. She could envisage a sustained effort on her part that would get her to her final goal.

Desirability

To achieve the outcome will take commitment and enthusiasm. Before you start, cross check that the efforts you will put in are worth the rewards of achieving your outcome.

First step

Another characteristic of the leader is that when their outcome is compelling they take action. They not only know the first step towards their outcome, they take it. Christabel Pankhurst made her speech in the middle of the campaign. She had already taken the first step.

A well-formed outcome, which is compelling at one time, can change. We know that the Pankhursts were flexible in terms of the actions they took during the First World War. It also may have been that the discussions around the Edwardian table about the outcome may have moved from the more liberal but inconceivable concept of universal suffrage for men and women to the more conceivable one of votes for the taxpayers.

Flexibility to adjust the outcome can be supported if the overarching outcome remains clear. The outcome may not be achieved without hiccups or changes and alterations, and the clarity of the image of the outcome is the magnetic pull that will guide great leaders, and you, towards achieving their goals.

 It is a mistake to look too far ahead. Only one link in the chain of destiny can be handled at a time.

Winston Churchill

Progress now

You can use this process for yourself to check how well formed your outcomes are.

State your outcome in the positive

_____

_____

_____

What will you see, hear and feel when you achieve it?

_____

_____

_____

What is the context in which it will be achieved? When, where and with whom?

_____

_____

_____

How will this fit with your life? What will be the effect on the rest of your life and others' lives? Is this acceptable to you?

_____

_____

_____

What holds you back at present? What stops you? What is your secondary gain and are the benefits greater if you act? How can you overcome these barriers or take these gains into your future outcome?

_____

_____

_____

What are the internal and external resources you need to achieve your outcome? Are these up to you and maintained by you?

_____

_____

_____

57

CASE STUDY

ROBBIE KEANE SCORES IN THE 92ND MINUTE: WORLD CUP FIFA 2002

He had a sense of it. Just a feeling. Strikers are like that sometimes, but by the 92nd minute it was unbearable. He knew he was going to score, but maybe the gods didn't.

'Against the Germans I knew that it was coming. Just as the game was going on it got worse. It was like a film in my head. I said to Quinny that I knew he was going to come on and he'd flick one on to me. When I saw he was coming on I knew that was it. When I scored I realized that it had been in my head. Saudi

Arabia, same thing. Just hope I get a few more of those feelings. Quinny couldn't have placed the header any better for me, even when I imagined him doing it.'

When you are a striker and this is your business, your bread and butter, sometimes you kick the ball and you just know that the netting will bulge and the crowd will rise and the old somersaults will be required. Against Germany, though, it happened so quick.

'The feeling was there and when Quinny headed it down it came off my stomach and fell well for me. Kahn was on fire all night and it looked like nothing would go past him. I'd had an overhead shot before that and I fell back a bit for that and missed it when I should have scored. I saw Kahn coming out this time, he comes out very fast and he looks huge. So I kept coming and I just hit it. He even got a hand to that. Sometimes you need the bit of luck. It hit the post and went in.'

Irish Times 15 June 2002

CHAPTER 4

The Building Blocks of Leadership

Excellence is not an act but a habit.

ARISTOTLE

Personally I'm always ready to learn although I do not like always being taught.

WINSTON CHURCHILL

WHAT PRESUPPOSES US TO BELIEVE THE TECHNIQUES WORK?

Organizations who model what other organizations do and then adapt it for their own use call it 'best practice'. Rank Xerox, Motorola and Rover Cars have all successfully used best practice to improve their productivity. The techniques we explore are developed from modelling high performers and great leaders – Winston Churchill, Ernest Shackleton, Mahatma Gandhi, Martin Luther King, Abraham Lincoln and John F. Kennedy – and also from the many leaders in organizations who have given us examples of excellent leadership practice on a smaller scale.

The following ideas are the bedrock that form the sound foundations for the rest of the chapters. By understanding these ideas you will have maximum gain from what follows. We believe that these ideas are valuable because of our success in using them with leaders in our development and coaching practice. As the ideas work for us, and for others with whom we work, we believe them to be true unless someone else proves them to be untrue.

If one can, anyone can

In the 1950s it was a common belief that man could not run a mile in less than four minutes. Roger Bannister did not hold this belief and he broke the four-minute barrier. Once broken, others found the inner belief to break the four-minute barrier over and over again. 'If Bannister can, I can.' Never underestimate the power of 'I can'. The choice is yours – we believe all people have the necessary resources to make any change they really want.

There is no failure, only feedback

I choose life over death . . . and if I should fail, then I will try again. The only true failure would be not to explore at all.

Shackleton

If you do not achieve the outcome you want, do something else and persist.

You use the feedback to discover what you need to change to succeed, and keep changing until you achieve what you want.

Thinking of failure is not helpful. If we fail at one thing and focus on the failure it is but a small step to believe we are failures . . .

and if we fail a few times, and keep focusing on what isn't working we create a self-fulfilling prophecy that we are a 'total' failure in all things. Our energy flows where attention goes. The remarkable results that are achieved in a so-called 'failing school' by dedicated teachers is often based on creating success in small matters with the children that turn into a big success overall.

The most flexible leader will control the system

Leaders who succeed display flexibility in their behaviour. They change what they do – and thus the response they get – as outside factors change. Leaders who do not succeed in the long term, though they may in the short term, maintain a consistent pattern of behaviour. Margaret Thatcher was successful using a domineering authoritarian style. Times changed, and the country and her followers required a different style. She did not believe it necessary, or chose not, to change. She was unceremoniously dropped by her senior colleagues and the Conservative Party.

Leaders who are inflexible will state the system and/or others need to change. Flexible leaders change themselves and thus change the response they get from others.

If you always do what you have always done, you always get what you have always got

Effective leaders learn from their experience, and if what they are doing does not work, do something else that moves them towards their outcome. Shackleton was a master of being flexible and changing what was happening. On the trip towards Elephant Island he changed his plans four times – first from heading towards Elephant Island to the east, to aiming for King George Island to the west, to trying for Hope Bay to the south west, and back to Elephant Island. The effective leader recognizes that persisting with old behaviour gets them nowhere – except for the place they do not want to be!

The final presupposition we wish to share in this chapter, a belief that affects the way you behave, is one which gives you the confidence to be able to successfully implement the learning that follows, to understand what is said and be able to make whatever changes you need to in your behaviour.

I'm in charge of my mind and therefore my behaviour

Many people act as if they are not in charge – other people make them do things or make things happen to them, or it is always someone or something else's fault.

Imagine if Nelson Mandela sat in Robbin's Island and said, 'There's nothing I can do, the forces of apartheid are too strong', or Abraham Lincoln sat in the White House and stated that, 'We can't do anything about slavery. It's better just to split the country in two', or William Wilberforce, who campaigned for abolition of slavery in the British Empire, said 'The economic forces that make slavery inevitable are too strong.'

If these great leaders had made these statements, they would have been at **effect**. They would have been made powerless by others. Instead they were at **cause**. Each believed they could cause things to change, and they did using all of the techniques that follow.

You have read five of the presuppositions of effective leadership here. You will meet others later in the text.

THE THREE-MINUTE LEADERSHIP SEMINAR

The short version of the key to effective leadership is that if you wish to be an effective leader you should:

- Have a very clear notion of the outcome you want to achieve and keep it in focus

- Be aware and alert so you notice how you move towards the outcome

- Have the flexibility to change what you do, and keep changing until you achieve your outcome.

If you don't know where you are going you may end up somewhere else. You learned how to set outcomes that were compelling in Chapter 3. The skill of awareness is knowing where to place your attention and how to make sense of the enormous quantity of data that is available to you every day.

Flexibility is the ability to change if your awareness indicates that you are not achieving your outcomes. You may not get straight to your outcome in the manner you first imagined. Your course may be zig-zagging and if you choose to persist and adapt to the circumstances you find you will still get to your well-formed outcome by whatever path it takes.

AWARENESS FOR LEADERSHIP

This section gives you more understanding of how effective leaders become aware, how they demonstrate high acuity skills, and how they notice what is happening as events and people move towards the outcome.

> The range of what we think, do, and achieve is limited by what we fail to notice. And because we fail to notice what it is that we fail to notice then there is little we can do to change . . . until we notice how failing to notice shapes our thoughts and deeds.
>
> John Grinder

Progress now

Awareness in action

When leading a team meeting, Joyce observed the following behaviours and she made the following interpretation: looking closely at the decriptions do you agree with her views?

George is looking down to his right, his face muscles are slack and his breathing is shallow.

Safraz is sitting back in his chair, with his legs stretched out before him, his hands behind his head, and is breathing slowly and deeply, with his eyes raised.

Bill is sitting hunched forward, with his arms crossed and his hands tightly holding his arms. Bill's eyes are down.

Joyce's view

George is depressed.

Safraz knows all the answers, he's confident and understands what's happening.

Bill is under threat.

How to be aware as a leader

Joyce has sensed how her followers have responded to her leadership behaviours. She has made a judgement about the impact she has had and has observed her followers closely and accurately. Yet her understanding may be faulty.

We could argue that the communication comes only through the words that are spoken. We might expect Bill to say 'those ideas threaten me', and Safraz to say 'I fully understand where you are going.' We must question whether George would say that he's depressed!

The words do not convey the full meaning. Ray Birdwhistle conducted a series of experiments at the University of Pennsylvania that conclude only 7 per cent of meaning in communication comes from words, 38 per cent comes from the voice, and 55 per cent from the body movement.

If we are to accurately interpret what the message is – the meaning of the communication – we need to pay attention to:

- *Body movements* (posture, gestures, breathing, facial expressions, eye movements, muscle and skin colour changes)
- *Voice* (tones, accents, stresses, pauses, intonation, rhythm and pitch)
- *Words* (the precise language used).

The body

Four main areas to observe are body posture, gestures and movement, skin tone and texture. The signs which give the most information are:

- **Breathing** – Observe whether the person breathes in their chest or stomach.

- **Colour changes** – When someone's face reddens it is often from anger, embarrassment or energy shift.

- **Muscle changes** – Muscle change is often around the mouth, a tight smile or minute grimace. Foreheads and eyes crease (and uncrease). You can notice when people are gritting their teeth, tensing their shoulders or jiggling their keys.

- **Mouth changes** – Observe changes in colour, skin tightness, and lip shape, edges, texture and swelling.

Voice

Tone

When someone says 'thank you' it can be a genuine 'thank you for your help', or a 'so thank you for giving me even more work'. The voice tone is significant in communication. As the voice changes the individual's state will change. The changes to hear are volume, pitch, rhythms, tempo, clarity and resonance.

Words

Words have meaning. Often the precise meaning is known only by the speaker. The listener interprets and can make an incorrect interpretation. If you are not listening to the tone the irony of the thank you can be missed. To get at the deeper meaning, you can ask, 'What specifically do you mean by . . . ?' Other examples of precision language are discussed in Chapter 6.

RAPPORT

Rapport is the process of establishing and maintaining a relationship between two or more people that facilitates and creates a desired response from the other person. Without rapport we cannot communicate effectively and without influential communication, we cannot lead.

Only if you have high level rapport skills can you lead using the techniques in Chapters 5 to 8. You know when you have rapport – when you and the person you are with are on the same wavelength and ideas flow, and you listen and are listened to.

We cannot communicate effectively without rapport. If you have a relationship with someone that is comfortable and easy both parties are more likely to listen. We explore below how to make it so. If you are uneasy you are unlikely to communicate comfortably.

How to build rapport

We do things to build rapport. It doesn't just happen. The key process in rapport building is **matching**. People who are in rapport tend to match or align with each other in a number of ways. In broad terms we match with all elements of communication – words, body posture and voice.

Words

We match words by matching how the other person presents the words. We match on:

- ❧ Length of phrase and sentence
- ❧ Key words in phrase (including jargon)
- ❧ Common experience and memories
- ❧ How others describe their experiences – do they describe pictures, tell stories, or give feelings?

Body posture

This gives us many choices for matching. We can match:

- ❧ Leg positions – legs crossed, stretched out, resting on knee, desk or any other position
- ❧ Head – tilt, down, to side, up
- ❧ Breathing – through chest or stomach, speed, depth
- ❧ Movements – of hands, legs, fingers and body
- ❧ Arm position – folded (which arm is on top), close to body/wide

Voice – tone/pitch, pace/volume, language

 Eyes – blink rate.

Matching

When you wish to be in rapport the objective is to be similar, to match the other person in the categories identified above.

As you learn how matching works, pick one body match only. When the follower folds their arms, fold your arms. As you get more comfortable choose another thing to match. Match their breathing. When the breathing speed changes follow the speed . . . and so on.

Always bear in mind your outcome is to build rapport. When you first try to match, you may begin to mimic, grossly following each movement. If this mimicking becomes obvious it may be insulting. Matching should be done step by step at an appropriate pace. You should never mimic (unless your outcome is to insult!).

Using rapport

The process of using rapport contains three stages: Match – Pace – Lead.

Begin by matching and then pace the individual by matching until you are comfortable with a level of rapport. If you then start to slowly change what you are doing, the other person will follow. If you have good rapport you will see the other person begin to follow the changed behaviour. When you have led and then have followed, you can begin to introduce the new ideas and thought pattern that you want them to follow.

Progress now

You have already practised your awareness skills, so you are able to notice changes more easily in others. In this exercise you will develop your skills in matching, pacing and leading using your voice.

1   Choose an unimportant situation. Pick a context where there is little at stake, such as a meeting over coffee with a colleague or a stranger in a public place. You will learn more if the other person does not know what is happening.

2   Match their voice – its pace, volume, tone, pitch. As you talk adjust your voice until it is similar to those of people nearby. Notice what happens

to the communication – easier or more difficult? Have you a feeling of rapport?

3   Now mismatch – alter your voice so that it is different from the others'. Increase your volume, pace, tone or pitch. Notice the impact on the communication – easier or more difficult? What has happened to the feeling of rapport?

If you have established rapport quickly in stage 2, you may find a dramatic and noticeable change at stage 3 as you have taken away from the other person a good feeling, rapport, that they enjoy.

4   Now return to matching. Change back to matching volume, pace, tone or pitch and notice how the smooth flow of communication returns.

Once you have demonstrated to yourself the power of rapport in voice matching, practise on the other elements of words and body posture.

As you become more expert, and matching becomes easier and easier, you will begin to combine the three elements of voice, body posture and words.

When you are comfortable with your ability to create rapport through matching and pacing, test the level of rapport by leading – in voice, body posture and language. When you have led, and the other has followed, you will be able to lead towards your leadership outcome. Be surprised, when you have rapport, how easily you can lead and others will follow.

SUCCESS WITH RAPPORT

Robert attended a three-day training programme in leadership skills that included rapport building. Robert was the managing director of a company that imported goods from the Far East and was about to leave on a major purchasing trip. Three days into the trip he sent this fax to the other course members:

'First of all the big news – I can confirm to you hand on heart – the leadership skills worked! No doubt before leaving I set out my targets for the trip – the clear goals identifying the best possible outcomes I could hope for on the trip. I was going to meet a manufacturer I had been trying to persuade to supply me for four years. Not only did I meet every one of those objectives in the first three days, I also saved a further US$80,000 which I had been prepared to pay up front for the parts moulds for the new product. This is the first time ever in my experience that my business did not have to pay these upfront charges – yet before I got there I would have considered this impossible, and certainly did not include it as a target outcome. I used rapport, matching, pacing and leading as we were taught, and paid particular attention to my listening skills to monitor the reactions I was getting. I felt things were going so well I dared to make more demands of the manufacturer than I would ever have contemplated in the past, and everything worked! It was so easy I floated on clouds in brilliant blue skies all weekend.'

How we learn – the 4Mat system

Bernice McCarthy developed 4Mat after she had explored many other learning styles. 4Mat moves us through a learning style and incorporates four combinations. We need to be taught in all four ways in order to be comfortable and successful while being stretched to develop other learning. We all have different learning preferences and learn more easily at one or two of the stages below. The four preferences are:

- ◊ **Why?** Why are we learning this piece of information? What are the benefits?

- ◊ **What?** What is it? What is the theory, the understanding?

- ◊ **How?** How do we do it? The experience of trying it out.

- ◊ **What if?** What if this, what if that, how can we apply it!

Progress now

Self Exercise on 4Mat

1   When you do not learn well it may be that one piece of the pattern was missing. Reflect on something that you needed to learn recently. Recall what happened. Were any stages left out?

2   Design a learning session for another using the four stages of Why?, What?, How? and What If? It may be coaching or mentoring someone through a skill that they have to follow. In your design you may reflect on the instruction for rapport building that followed the format of why, what, how and what if. You will find it useful to begin with a one-line 'mini-what' to give people a label or title for the session and give them some idea of the area for learning. An example of a 4Mat learning cycle is:

- Mini-what is 'now we would like to explore the topic of rapport building':

- Why is having rapport important to you?

- What? – detail of the components of rapport

- How? – a demonstration of rapport building and a chance to practise it in pairs

- What if? – a question and answer session.

3   Observe the increased effectiveness of the learning and leading when using the format system to explain something.

- Understanding your own learning preferences is useful.
  Understanding others' style can be an important aid to matching and building rapport and getting them to be able to take on your ideas.

Further reading

Bodenhauser, Bob and Hall, Michael, 1999, *The User's Manual to the Brain*, The Cromwell Press, Wiltshire.

CHAPTER 5
The Beliefs of a Leader

The most effective leaders are those who first learn to lead themselves.

JIM KOUZES AND BARRY POSNER, *THE LEADERSHIP CHALLENGE*

When you see a worthy person, endeavour to emulate him. When you see an unworthy person, then examine your inner self.

CONFUCIUS

Let me assert my firm belief that the only thing we have to fear is fear itself.

F.D. ROOSEVELT

BELIEFS

■ They can because they think they can.

Virail

The actions that you take as a leader are influenced greatly by the beliefs that you hold. A belief is a generalization about yourself and/or the world. Your beliefs are what you take to be true at any moment. They guide you in perceiving and interpreting your reality. Beliefs may be strongly held and they may enable you to act, or not. Beliefs are not cast in stone, they are only something that you have put together in your mind and so, where they are not helpful to you, beliefs can be changed. Beliefs can be enabling: they can help achieve success in leadership – or they can be limiting: holding you back from the success that you can achieve.

Enabling beliefs

 If you believe you can or believe you can't, you are probably right.

Henry Ford

In a recent coaching session, we were fascinated to hear from a leader in community development who stated that one of her underlying beliefs is 'You can – you just have to find the way'. She applies this when working with communities that others have written off in the belief that nothing will work. Because others hold this belief, the sort of thinking that can unearth a solution is never applied. This community leader holds the belief that every community can achieve significant things in the ways that are right for them. Consequently, she believes it is worth spending energy and time working with residents to find out what will work and then working with other agencies with influence to back their proposals.

Powerful beliefs can take people to places that they otherwise would not go.

Michael Jordan the basketballer believed, 'I never looked at the consequences of missing a big shot . . . when you think about the consequences, you always think of a negative result.'

Nelson Mandela when in prison said, 'If you want to make peace with your enemy, you have to work with your enemy. Then he becomes your partner.'

'You can do anything when you believe in it, that's why I need to go back.'

Shackleton

Consider the beliefs of Churchill who in 1930, wrote 'Don't be content with things as they are. The earth is yours and the fullness thereof. Enter upon your inheritance, accept your responsibilities. Raise the glorious flags again, advance then upon your new enemies. . . . Don't take no for an answer. Never submit to failure. Do not be fobbed off with mere personal success or acceptance. You will make all kinds of mistakes; but as long as you are generous and true and also fierce . . .'

Beliefs are the bedrock of someone's behaviour. Imagine that Churchill did not hold these beliefs, or he held other ones, what would have happened then? He may have even had a day when he did or did not hold a particular belief. We can all recall a time when we just didn't hold one of our normal beliefs and it will have really affected our behaviour on that day.

Imagine what it would be like if you had said the things that Churchill said. Imagine what would be different in your leadership right now if you chose to take on some of the beliefs that are in Churchill's statement. You would not take 'No' for an answer, you would find a way to influence to get the 'Yes' answer you want, you would not accept failure; you would go for success. You are able to presuppose that Churchill's belief was yours for a moment or longer as it suits you. As you read this you might like to 'act as if' you held the belief and experience the difference it would make to your actions. If you like the difference, you could wear it, like a jacket, for a little longer, until you may find it is integrated into all that you do and has a benefit to you and those around you in the long term. If at any time holding the belief that you have taken on from someone else no longer feels congruent, you can then decide to put it down.

Progress now

What do you believe are the things that you can do? Write below your top five beliefs about you as a leader.

🍃 _____

🍃 _____

🍃 _____

🍃 _____

🍃 _____

These beliefs are likely to underpin all sorts of things that you do and achievements that you have already made. They are the sorts of things that others might want to copy from you, the way of being who you are that you already have and that others admire.

LIMITING BELIEFS

A belief can be very enabling; however, a limiting belief can have the opposite effect and hold us back from doing something.

■ The ideal is in thyself; the impediment, too, is in thyself.

Thomas Carlyle

If you accept that a belief is something that you have constructed for yourself and that those beliefs that do not serve you well can be reconstructed to be more useful, then you have a powerful tool to increase your effectiveness as a leader.

Think about a belief that is true for you that you consider holds you back. Now think about someone you admire who does not hold this belief and is more able or resourceful because of this different belief. Imagine what it would be like if you held their beliefs. After the next example of this in action, you will do an exercise that demonstrates the power of imagining.

Pamela and Moira

An example of the power of holding different beliefs is evident where Pamela holds the belief that 'people are out to get her and put her down'. This limits Pamela in all sorts of circumstances. She feels unable to trust others and she is not willing to do anything until she thinks it is perfect. This results in her spending long periods of time behind her desk, mulling over all the pitfalls and guarding herself against anyone who may come into the room. Her guarded welcome to visitors is often matched by a guarded response. When people do give her feedback she is constantly looking for the negative intention in what they have said or imagining the significance of what they have not said. Although Pamela's positive intention in holding this belief is to protect herself from harm or harsh criticism, it really does hold her back. Pamela creates her own reality.

Her colleague Moira, however, holds the belief that 'people really want to hear her ideas and they want her to do well'. Any feedback or criticism they give Moira is just to help her get better at what she is doing. Consequently, Moira is willing to express and share her ideas at an early stage, which allows her to refine her ideas and performance as she goes along. She has her door open, welcomes people who pop in and talks with enthusiasm about the ideas she is developing. There is a regular buzz of conversation coming from her office. Because Moira believes feedback is valuable, she invariably thanks people for the comments they make which, in turn, makes them feel good about giving her comments. This sets up a virtuous circle of feedback and improvement. The people who have given feedback or criticism then feel involved in Moira's performance and applaud the improvements she makes and her end results. Moira, like Pamela, creates her own reality.

What would it be like if Pamela took on the beliefs of Moira for just one project. Pamela could, for the purposes of this exercise, presuppose that Moira's beliefs were her own and then act accordingly. She would be acting as if she was Moira, and thinking through: What would Moira do in this situation? How would she approach this? How would she feel about expressing her ideas and getting comments back that will improve her performance? What words does Moira use to thank others for their comments and criticisms? Pamela can then act as if she was Moira and experience all the differences inside herself as she accepts comments as being valuable; feels good about herself as she shows flexibility in considering ideas which may then spark off more ideas of her own; and be confident in the belief that comments are given because others want her to do well and achieve her potential. Pamela, holding these beliefs, would act in an entirely different way with her own new virtuous circle of experience, which would be a very resourceful thing to do. After she has done this, she may realize she could take this choice wherever she chooses in the future.

Progress now

You, like Pamela can adopt other beliefs. This exercise allows you to try out a belief that is serving someone else well as a leader. When you have experienced the usefulness of the new belief then you can expand the exercise to include more, or exchange some of your beliefs that may be holding you back.

- Think of an admired other person.
- List the beliefs they hold that serve them well in the kind of situation you are thinking about.
- 'Act as if' you, too, hold these beliefs for the period of the project you wish to do.
- Now that you can presuppose these beliefs to be true, what can you see yourself doing, hear yourself saying, and what feelings do you get as a result of these changes?
- Note how you are free to do things in a different way and the new choices that this gives you.
- Note what you are free from.

Doing this exercise allows you to give yourself more choice, and have access to more resources. You can then choose if you want to hold any of these beliefs for a longer period of time. To do this you may now want to consider how this new belief fits in with other beliefs that you already hold.

LEVELS OF INFLUENCE

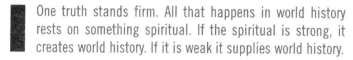

One truth stands firm. All that happens in world history rests on something spiritual. If the spiritual is strong, it creates world history. If it is weak it supplies world history.

Schweitzer

There are different levels of change and influence. It is apparent that some changes, which are well intentioned and even generous, do not always change what really happens. They may be operating at the wrong level.

CASE STUDY

Someone like **James** may already be familiar to you. James was determined to make a change in how his career was going. He didn't see himself as a high flyer but he definitely thought he might be able to improve his chances by doing something positive. He changed his office around, went to a colour consultant and bought new clothes, he bought a computer and had classes in IT, and even bought some 'high impact' motivational tapes and yet still there was no substantial change either in James or in what happened to him and he was heard to say 'I knew it wouldn't work for me'.

James had made changes to his environment (changing his office and buying a new computer), he had changed some behaviours (dressed differently) and even improved his skills and capabilities (learned to use IT), but the change in his life and how he felt about himself did not alter, because he had not attended to the more powerful influences of beliefs about himself ('I knew it wouldn't work'), identity ('I am not a high flyer') and purpose ('what is the higher reason for doing things').

Everyone's world is made up of many different influences or levels. Leadership involves co-ordinated changes of yourself and others across different levels at different times to create the world that you as a leader envisage. These levels can be shown in the following way to illustrate a hierarchy of influence.

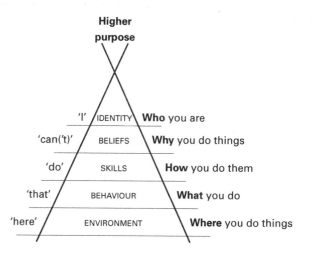

Higher purpose

'I'	IDENTITY	**Who** you are
'can('t)'	BELIEFS	**Why** you do things
'do'	SKILLS	**How** you do them
'that'	BEHAVIOUR	**What** you do
'here'	ENVIRONMENT	**Where** you do things

Levels of influence

In working through this technique, you will be invited to consider what drives you on and what holds you back. You can then choose to make changes that will improve your effectiveness and sense of alignment as a leader: it is a rewarding experience that can have some real benefits for you and for others.

At the very top of this model is the level of *mission* that represents the wider purpose in your life. For some, this is a sort of spirituality or wider reason for life. It is at this level that mission and vision statements are expressed.

Then there is the level that represents **who** you are. The *identity* level. The 'I am' or the 'I am not' statements. I am a fighter or I am a pacifist. Your role and sense of self are held at this level.

Any process is influenced by the *beliefs and values* that people hold. Beliefs about what is so and not so, about what is right and not right, about what can be and what can't. It is the **why** of leadership. These beliefs are often imprinted early in your life and they do not have to remain unchanged forever! Sometimes they will serve you well and at other times they will hold you back.

People have refined *capabilities* that are well-honed clusters of behaviours that fit together to allow them to do things in a way that is effective and almost effortless and second nature. They are the **how**; how things are done.

The individual actions that people take make up another level that is described as *behaviour.* Different people behave in different ways and take actions that will not be the same as yours. **What** people do is fascinating. The capabilities of the communicator can be broken down into behaviours, for example listening, chatting, speech, use of language.

Finally, look for the **where and when**, the *environment* and the physical places. This environment also indicates the **who else** is involved: your competition, the market, your customers or your community.

So, starting at the base, consider what you need to change or pay attention to at this level. Are you operating in the right environment? Have you created the right environmental conditions in the light of all that is in the levels above it? For instance, if you hold a belief that all staff have a valuable part to play in your enterprise, does this reflect itself in the environment you provide for them to work in?

There is a natural hierarchy in these levels. Each level above is more abstract and more powerful than those below and has a greater degree of impact on those below. A change at an upper level will cascade and permeate through those below it. A change at a lower level may influence those above and it may not. Lower level changes are definitely not as powerful as higher level changes.

Good leaders ensure attention is paid to every level in this model. To bring about the world that you want others to subscribe to, you need alignment through all the levels. The most powerful impact will be felt by things being right at the top, but that is no excuse to neglect the bottom.

James's voice analysis

James had made changes at the lower end levels of environment, behaviour and a little at skill and capability level. However, he has clearly not addressed how he holds his own identity and beliefs. When he changes these, for example, from 'I am not a high flyer' to something like 'I am an emergent leader', everything below can begin to change and realign to support this identity.

Here is an exercise to run through for yourself to see where your leadership could benefit from some finer alignment and tuning.

Progress now

What is your vision or mission and what is the relationship to the wider purpose or system that you operate within?

My mission as a leader is to _____

_____

What is your identity or role in relation to this vision and mission?

I am a leader because I am _____

_____

What key beliefs and values are encapsulated in your vision and mission?

The values that are important in my leadership are _____

_____

The beliefs that support me in leading others are _____

_____

What capabilities and skills will you use to accomplish your vision and mission and what behaviours will be indicators that you are doing this?

My capabilities as a leader are _____

_____

What particular behaviours will be evident when all this is in tune and working well?

The behaviours that are evident and support my leadership are

_____

_____

In what context and environment will you do this?

I am a leader in the context of _____

_____

These are the things I will get right in my environment ____

_____

For many people reading this statement from top to bottom will give a clear picture of the path that they intend to follow.

As you read yours, you will be aware of anything that does not ring true and be able to revisit and adjust your statement until it hits just the right note.

MANAGE YOUR STATE – MANAGE YOUR OUTCOME

■ Leadership is more a state than an activity.

Gilles Pajou

Lucy was a successful manager of a Leisure Centre. She was able to manage a complex business that operated 360 days a year, seven days a week and 18 hours a day. Lucy had respect from staff, customers and the elected Councillors who oversaw the services. Lucy also had 'up days' and 'down days'. She had to make a presentation to representatives from all the clubs and societies that used the busy sports centre. She had been asked to convince them of a new programming balance that was being introduced to allow more access to services for the general public. Before the meeting Lucy was operating out of 'down day' mode. What was printable of her language included 'They will never believe me', 'I hate doing presentations' and 'I shouldn't be making this presentation – can't someone else do it?' Her posture was slumped, her energy low, her pace of voice slow and generally not oozing confidence. You can imagine how her address went down.

Wouldn't it be fantastic to have a process that enables you and Lucy to turn a down day into an up day and be in the best possible state to deal with any situation that you have to face? Sportspeople are very good at achieving this state of being to aid peak performance and as leaders we can learn a great deal from them.

Having a great day

Dennis Lillee, the great Australian cricketer and fast bowler, used to show that he had days when everything clicked and worked brilliantly. For him it was only a very occasional experience to sense that things would not produce the results that he and others expected of him. He knew he was highly capable as a fast bowler, and he also knew that he had to get himself into the right state of mind and body to produce high performance cricket by the start of play. Sometimes this was a matter of physical well-being but more often it was a matter of mental state and self-belief, or lack of it, that made the difference. Lillee had special gestures that seemed to set him up for peak performance, such as a characteristic rub of the ball as he turned to run in and bowl.

No sporting icon can afford the luxury of too many 'down' days — and the sporting public would certainly not be tolerant of that.

Creating a state for peak performance

How do we attain a state for peak performance? In Lillee's example you need the capability from talent and practice. Nevertheless up days and down days still exist. How can you have many more up days, and in particular be able to produce the performances that will make all the difference when it really matters?

Anchoring

Lillee may have instinctively used a process called anchoring as he rubbed the ball. Sportspeople use it all the time. Wimbledon 2002 finalist Leighton Hewitt said, 'Every time I step onto the Wimbledon Court, I take my positive memories with me.' The step onto the court is the anchor.

Anchoring is when an external stimulus triggers an internal emotional state. The trigger can be through any one of the senses. The sound of a song (external stimulus) takes you straight back to feelings (internal emotional state) you had about someone or somewhere the first time you heard it. The sound of the crowd triggers the memory and feeling of winning the last match. A visual anchor might be a photograph or a picture, a view of someone's face or even a colour that has significance. Seeing an image, such as a house where you used to live, can unlock strong associated feelings with being there.

Positive and negative anchors can be set up. Positive ones can create 'up' days and negative ones 'down' days. The most extreme negative anchors are known as phobias. We look at dealing with phobias in Chapter 11.

Creating great feelings

How could you create positive states for your leadership equivalent of a big sporting arena? Perhaps you want to feel confident just before making a presentation. This is how you connect a positive internal feeling to a unique but replicable external stimulus (a gesture, sound or anchor) that you can use any time you want the feeling of confidence.

Progress now

An anchor for confidence

1 Choose a state that you want to have at your disposal, something you really want. We will use confidence as an example.

2 Choose an anchor or gesture that is unique and that you can do easily and discreetly. An example would be squeezing your wrist.

3 Recall a time when you had confidence. Re-experience fully that sensation of confidence and as you do and it begins to feel really good, create your anchor by squeezing your wrist.

4 Hold the squeezed wrist for a few seconds and remove it just before the feeling begins to subside.

5 Think about something else for a minute (like what you had for breakfast).

6 Test your anchor by making the gesture (squeezing your wrist) and re-experiencing the positive feeling of confidence that now comes with it. You have just set off your anchor!

7 Now re-print this link between internal emotional feeling (confidence) with this external stimulus (squeezing your wrist) by repeating steps 2 to 5. Do this at least five times to make the link really strong.

> **8**   Now, think about the next time you need to feel confident. As you
> imagine this scenario set off your anchor (squeeze your wrist) and you
> now have the feeling of being in that future situation with your
> confidence. Notice how much better it feels.

You now have a process for anchoring. It is valuable to you and it
is a valuable coaching tool for you to help get peak performance
from others.

Lessons for Lucy

One of the major factors that has allowed Lucy to move on in her
career has been her ability to manage her state and to get
himself into the frame of mind and body that she needs to
convince others (and herself) to follow the strategic social plans
that she now implements. Her career may never have progressed
beyond the leisure centre without this skill in state management.

Getting others ready for peak performance

As a leader you can also coach others through this process to
help them be in the resourceful state that would be needed for
peak performance. Your ability to lead is greatly enhanced by
techniques that you can apply to others to get them in a state to
perform at their peak. What a gift to be able to give someone.

DEALING WITH INTERNAL CONFLICT

 A leader who doesn't hesitate before he sends his nation into battle is not fit to be a leader.

Golda Meir

Lucy is now able to generate a resourceful state and yet at a deeper level she still isn't performing they way she wants to. She said 'A part of me wants to take risks and a part of me doesn't'. Her statement allows us to see that there can almost be a competition going on within ourselves, and that when such a sense of competing intentions and motivations exists it can lead to a sense of tension within yourself.

In any situation that you face, you also face the possibility of having an internal dilemma about what will be the best course of action to take. When you consider this dilemma you may notice that one part of you says that you should go ahead and take the action that you are thinking of, while another part is cautioning care and asking you to hold back. There may even be another part or voice that starts to nag you about your inability to make a decision.

Your internal world will be familiar to you, and probably quite strange to others. Some successful leaders have talked in coaching sessions about the parts that they have. Sometimes there are two or three that are clearly evident to them, and we have worked with one successful international marketing executive who definitely had seven.

So let's look at these and work through a process that can help you come to decisions that feel right and allow you to skip the agitating and time-wasting processes that may currently be restraining you.

The following exercise may, at first reading, seem a little unusual to some people, and not to others, so we would like you to suspend judgement for a moment and work your way to the end of the exercise where you will realize just how helpful this may be.

Progress now

Resolving internal conflict

This six-step process will allow you to generate more choices in your behaviours. It uses the principle of separating the behaviour from the intention.

Step 1. Ask the part that objects to the behaviour what positive intention it has in making the objection. Just listen and then acknowledge that this intention is a valuable one, even if the way it is being expressed is not that helpful. You may want to give this part a label or a name for ease of reference. We will call it Part A (you will think of a name or label that is far more appropriate to you).

Step 2. Ask the part (Part B) that is proposing the behaviour what positive intention it has to you. Acknowledge and thank Part B for this intention – this will let you know the underlying motivation of Part B in doing what it is doing.

Step 3. Ask Part B to suggest other ways of achieving the outcome that it wants that takes account of which might satisfy Part A's positive intentions. Think of at least three, and say them out loud. (If you can't think of three, ask your creative part to make some suggestions.)

Step 4. Ask Part A if it is satisfied by any of these alternative behaviours and if it would be willing to go along with one of them for an agreed period of time, remembering that Part B has a positive intention in wanting to take this action. Keep the discussion going between the parts until they can agree.

Step 5. Now that these two parts have agreed, ask if there are any other parts that are not happy with the proposed behaviour. If there is, create and name Part C and go through steps 2, 3 and 4 until it too is happy to agree to the proposed behaviour.

Step 6. Now imagine yourself taking the new agreed step and experience in advance how it will feel and hear all the parts supporting it.

You will now feel very motivated to take this action and make it successful.

CHANGING HABITUAL REACTIONS FAST!

■ Winning is a habit. Unfortunately so is losing.

Vince Lombardi

Helen

'Every time it happens I react in the same way that gets me into trouble!' said Helen, a talented human resource manager with a quick and wicked wit that landed her in difficult situations more than once. On this occasion she had made a cutting and sarcastic remark about a member of the Executive team (Steve) who was absent at the time. Steve was a rich source of material for Helen as he was an innovative thinker. Helen's comment on this occasion was, 'Which part of NO does the intergalactic traveller not understand today.' Everyone laughed and yet it left an uneasy feeling as people left the room. 'What else might she say when they were absent – and who would laugh then?' they may have mused.

Stimulus begets response

We all run patterns that cause us to act in a predictable but unhelpful way. We have them ingrained as much in our home life as we do in our working situation. You know the ones – you come home and someone's question or tone of voice just seems to make you respond with an unhelpful comment or an unattractive voice tone all of your own. A sort of stimulus/response with no gap for thought occurs. Something just triggers you off and almost without helping yourself, you hear yourself making your standard type of response. Well you can change these reactions using a simple technique that enables leaders to choose a more helpful way of responding.

Changing your reaction in a 'swish'

A technique has been developed called 'swish' which allows you to choose the response behaviour you want to a particular stimulus, instead of being trapped into the response you have habitually given. Whether it is the HR Director Helen or yourself, your leadership can benefit from this technique.

Helen has a link between the image she creates in her head of Executive team member Steve, and the compulsion to make a joke. Every time she thought of his face, she heard herself making a sarcastic remark. We asked Helen to describe the moment she begins to formulate her comments when getting an image of Steve, then to fully re-experience making these remarks including the moment seconds later when she would cringe at what she had said. We asked her to make this image of her reacting to Steve big and bright, close, in focus. Then we asked her to make an image of her more resourceful type of reaction, one that she would be proud of in response to the stimulus of seeing his face in her mind. This image would be small, dark, and put in the far corner of the first picture. Helen was adamant that she did not want to look at the big bright picture as she was much more attracted to the smaller darker image.

We encouraged her to identify the behaviour in response to thinking of Steve that she thought would be more resourceful and helpful to her. Her response was to show people she was interested in them and to show genuine curiosity about what her unmet needs were. Because Helen's mind is now committed to this image that is small, dark and in one corner she may literally want to 'swish' the new behaviour image until it is programmed in as her new regular pattern. Between each state, make sure you clear state so you are ready to 'swish' again. Never swish in both directions or you literally will not know if you are coming or going.

Progress now

New behaviour swish

Bring to mind a pattern of yours that is habitual in response to a certain trigger or situation. Here are the steps you can follow:

1   Identify the unwanted behaviour or reaction that you wish to change and what triggers that behaviour or reaction.

2   Create a bright, associated, large image of the trigger behaviour. It may be an internal feeling that you can fully associate with or an external image where you fully re-experience the memory. Enrich this image with all the sub-detail that is there.

3   Now put that image aside and clear your mind.

4   Construct the preferred behaviour, how you would really like to respond, when the trigger occurs. Keep this image dissociated. Give this new image all the resources that you need to have in that situation. It will be an image of you being the sort of you that you really want to be. Make it compelling and realistic, and notice how this will fit with the rest of your life. Make sure this image remains dissociated at this point.

5   Put this image aside and clear your mind.

6   Bring back the big, bright associated image of the unwanted behaviour and put a frame around it. Place the small darker dissociated image of the desired behaviour in one corner.

7   Now swish the small image up and over the other image so that it completely floods your view with the image of the new desired behaviour. Now associate with this new behaviour. Repeat step 7 up to five times until it happens automatically and becomes your new automatic reaction.

This technique is a powerful and fast way to change a behaviour pattern that you currently have that limits you in your abilities to be an even more effective leader.

CHAPTER 6
Unlocking Patterns of Communication

The first task of a leader is to define reality.

MAX DEFREE, FORMER CHAIRMAN OF THE HERMANN
MILLER COMPANY

Nine tenths of wisdom consists of being wise in time.

THEODORE ROOSEVELT

When we understand the other fellow's viewpoint and he understands ours, then we can sit down and work out our differences.

HARRY S. TRUMAN

WHY CAN'T THEY UNDERSTAND?

Claudia, the CEO of an organization in the hospitality sector, had decided on a new mission statement. She decided on the phrase, 'Ladies and gentlemen serving ladies and gentlemen', adapted from the Ritz Carlton Group. She presented the statement of her mission as a challenge to her key staff to change the way they work. Her delivery was a well-crafted PowerPoint presentation, which she had worked on until 4 a.m. the previous morning. During the presentation she was concerned that the reaction she was getting was poor. Many of the staff seemed disinterested and unexcited. Indeed, the response to the presentation was disappointing. The negative comments were in the majority, with only one positive comment.

'Change makes me feel down. I'm never sure what is happening around here.'

'It's typical – a new statement of intent – and there won't be the training and communication to support it.'

'It's a typical glib presentation. Lots of pictures and noise and I can't get to grips with the change that is wanted so I don't think it will work.'

'What is wrong with what we have already been doing?'

(115)

'The change is just like all the other initiatives that we've seen – and they have all failed.'

'A superb and clear presentation. I can see exactly the way to success.'

She was disappointed in the response. Her message was meant to be inspirational and visionary and she felt frustrated by the inability of her staff to understand. Her managers echoed her frustration for they had run follow-up sessions for the staff and had heard similar responses.

THE LEADERSHIP COMMUNICATION MODEL

Contrary to what most chieftains think you are not remembered by what you did in the past, but by what most think you did.

Robert Weiss, *The Leadership Secrets of Attila the Hun*

Claudia will be able to understand much of what happened to her message if she understands the Leadership Communication Model. The model explains the processes of how messages are *deleted*, *distorted* and *generalized*, how you experience something inside yourself and how *internal representations* of events are created. How the phrase 'it makes me feel down' creates a negative state and may physically make the individual down. The Leadership Communication Model, developed by Stenhouse Consulting in Cardiff, is circular. The *external event* causes the *internal representation*, a meaningful pattern, which causes the recipient to behave in a certain way in the external world, which then affects the behaviour of the initial sender — which influences a further *external event*.

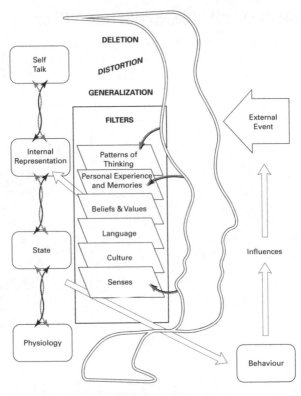

DELETION

DISTORTION

GENERALIZATION

FILTERS

Self
Talk

Internal
Representation

State

Physiology

Patterns of
Thinking

Personal Experience
and Memories

Beliefs & Values

Language

Culture

Senses

External
Event

Influences

Behaviour

118 **The leadership communication model**
(Source: Stenhouse consultancy, Cardiff)

The stages in the Leadership Communication Model are:

An external event occurs. The receiver uses their *senses*, eyes (visual), ears (auditory) and feeling (kinesthetic) to process the *external* event. Feelings are often further refined to include taste (gustatory) and smells (olfactory).

Psychological and communication research since the 1950s has shown us that there are so many external stimuli we could hardly begin to count them. Nevertheless our senses are remarkable and have enough receptors to take in about 11 million bits per second of information. Our conscious capacity to process information, however, is comparatively limited at 40 bits per second. An enormous reduction that demonstrates that most of the information is discarded before conscious processing occurs! And the conscious brain is limited in its capacity. Miller demonstrated the conscious mind could only hold seven (plus or minus two) pieces of data. Thus it is difficult to remember long telephone numbers unless we break them down into smaller chunks – national code, local code and individual number.

Progress now

Remember and write down what you heard in the last minute. Now listen really carefully for the next minute and write down things you hear. The second list will be longer than the first. You may now notice sounds outside – a car, a lawnmower, or inside – a tap running, a slight noise from the lights that you had previously deleted. If you do this in a group you will be amazed at the different things listed. You realize how much you normally delete from your conciousness so you can begin to make sense of the world.

DELETION

We delete much of what is available to us.

Deletion can be recognized at work. For instance after a meeting someone says, 'Give me a call about the new project on Wednesday in the afternoon. We need to discuss the costings, the equipment profile, the potential demand and the potential suppliers, particularly the choice between Jones, Smith and Williams. My internal number is 87642 and my email is . . .' The next morning you think, 'I must call — who was that? When? Afternoon or morning?' When there is too much data to remember precisely you take some action to record it — write it down or stop and create ways of remembering parts. For example, Smith and Jones are a comedy duo, so that's the supplier. There is also overload in the communication above. A memorable communication is, 'Phone me tomorrow afternoon about the project. Please have details on suppliers Jones, Smith and Williams'; six pieces of data that may be remembered. It is not the listener's job to wade through the morass of data and decide what the communicator believes important in the message.

GENERALIZATION

As well as deletion, you generalize to make sense of the world by putting events into classifications or categories. When the event or part of it seems to happen again you jump to the conclusion that it is going to be just like last time. For example, 'I once met a mathematician who was boring. Here is another mathematician, he must be boring too.'

A generalization is when you say, 'That's one of those so I will think of it as if it was one of those.' Examples of generalizations are:

Experience	Generalization
He's a salesman.	He's like all salesmen.
That's a technology company.	One technology company I know is innovative. It must be innovative.
He's over 65.	He's too old. He won't be computer literate.
He has created a mission statement.	He must be a leader. Leaders create mission statements.
He lost an argument.	He can't be a leader. People who lose arguments aren't leaders.

You do not need to explore cause and effect in the statements above. How the generalization is created is interesting but not critical. What is important is that there is a generalization created. What makes you regard the over-65 as computer illiterate is not important. That you do, whether it is true or not, is the effect of the generalization and the effect may be that he feels undervalued and demeaned when he is very computer literate. You behave based on the meaning to you of your generalization.

DISTORTION

Through the process of deletion and generalizing you *distort* the reality that is the external event. The distortion creates an inaccurate representation of the reality. Distortion is neither good nor bad, it is simply a process that you follow.

You may have a telephone number that you remember incorrectly because two numbers are transposed. You may normally remember the number incorrectly, and in your conscious brain correct it and dial it correctly. Occasionally you dial on 'auto pilot', unconsciously, and the wrong number is dialled. You may hear yourself say 'I often get that wrong' – a sure sign that the distortion is well embedded.

Distortion is also evident when the police take statements after an incident. People notice different things depending on the filter that they use, as discussed below. The effect is that the evidence often becomes – 'it was a van', 'a truck', 'a pick-up truck' and it was 'red', 'black', etc. Each individual has a different representation of the event. All are true to them.

HOW DO YOU DELETE, GENERALIZE AND DISTORT?

You delete, generalize and distort because you can't take in with accuracy everything you experience. You filter the external event to allow you to make sense of it: The filters are:

Patterns of thinking: how you sort, orient or size your experiences. As an example of what is termed a pattern of thinking, some people always look for the benefits of a change, the enjoyment of reaching goals, whereas others always look for the pitfalls and what could go wrong. Their internal response affects whether they are positive or negative in how they respond to change. Patterns of thinking are so important to the leader that we explore them in more detail in Chapter 7.

Personal experience and memories: what has happened to you before. If you hear a 'bang' as you are driving, and you have had a recent blowout, you are likely to have an internal representation of fear or concern and the memory of the flat tyre, and that causes you to pull over more quickly. An inexperienced driver may distort the sound, not hearing it for what it is, drive on and, if it was a blowout, ruin the tyre. The staff member who says that the 'change is like all the initiatives we've seen' will be working from her experience.

Belief and values: beliefs are the generalizations you make about the world, your operating principles about causality, meaning, others' behaviour and identity. Values in a wider sense are what are important to you and are supported by your beliefs. Values are what motivate you in life. At some level they drive what you do. Values relate your identity, as discussed in logical levels. You really care about them. They are the fundamental principles you operate by.

Language: you can give different meanings for words that alter the internal representation, for example, if you use the word 'challenge' to describe a project. A 'challenge' to one person may mean a threat. To another it may be an opportunity to excel. The response from the individual will depend on their view – whether they reject or welcome the new project.

Culture: the same behaviours may have different meaning depending on the culture of an organization or community or the cultural background of an individual. Culture derives from a complex interaction of values and beliefs. Language, common practice and gestures within a community reinforce culture. Unwritten laws apply.

Senses: the senses are how you perceive the external events — sight, sound, feel, smell, or taste. You each have differently developed senses. People with highly developed auditory senses are more likely to respond to sounds that the less developed will not hear. The same picture of a lake to someone with highly developed visual sense may be bright and panoramic with deep colours. To the less visually developed it may look like a flat sea.

Communication using the senses

How people talk about an event afterwards reflects their preferred sense for coding external events. Visual people say things like, 'I got a clear picture', 'You can see what she was saying', and 'She made her vision clear to me'. Auditory people might say, 'I heard his central points loud and clear', 'His ideas resonate with me', and 'He was clear as a bell'. A kinesthetic might say, 'I could really empathize', 'He feels deeply about his ideas', 'He is passionate about expressing them'.

One particular percentage breakdown for preferred represent-ation systems is 45 per cent visual, 35 per cent auditory and 20 per cent kinesthetic.

THE INTERNAL REPRESENTATION: THE CONSEQUENCE OF THE DELETIONS, DISTORTIONS AND GENERALIZATIONS?

■ A Hun's perception is reality to him.

Robert Weiss, *The Leadership Secrets of Attila the Hun*

The consequence of the process of deletion, distortion and generalizations creates a unique representation, an internal representation, of the world built on the individual's patterns, thinking, personal experience and memories, belief and values, language, cultural experience and senses.

The internal representation will differ between individuals. A story about spiders produces a different reaction in the arachnaphobe, than the spider expert. Staff watching Claudia present get different internal representations from her words. Some see her as competent, others as confusing. Therefore when asked to comment on her presentation they give different responses – 'Excellent, knows where she is going' or 'Woolly, unclear, doesn't know what she's at.' Yet both have had the same external experience – that of the presentation.

For any given external experience, you each generate different 'maps' that contain the bits that you notice, with your unique deletions, generalizations and distortions. The concept of 'maps' can be expanded to give you an insight into the way others view the world, and how individuals' maps affect what they perceive in the external world.

The effect of individuals' 'maps' gives rise to different responses. If a team is visiting another business, the accountant may experience issues the marketing people don't experience, and vice versa. You all have different 'maps' and yet often assume that there is only one 'map' – yours, and often argument is about forcing others to accept the 'truth' of your map. You must ask with your understanding of maps – is there a true map?

Understanding that you and your followers store 'maps' not the reality is a key to successful leadership, and is contained in possibly the most powerful presupposition – 'the map is not the territory'.

Progress now

Look down with your head slumped and eyes focused on the ground. Now remember a time when you felt really successful, really good and keep looking down, with your head slumped. You may have found looking down a difficult posture to maintain while having such positive thoughts. Usually when you are physiologically down, your state is a down one, and your internal representation will often be negative. A successful leader we know says 'lift' when she needs to be in a positive state. She changes her body posture to head high and shoulders square. She changes from a negative or neutral state to a positive one. This change affects her and it certainly affects those around her.

SELF-TALK

Self-talk is the final part of the model. So far the model has considered only external events that you filter. You can also generate internal representations from inside yourself. *Self-talk* or internal dialogue, the voice that often chats away to us, also affects the other three systems of sight, sound and feelings. The inner voice saying, 'I can do this', 'I can't do this', 'What if this happened?', 'I feel really insecure today' will affect all three systems. One other effect of self-talk is that it can block your awareness of external events. Indeed if your self-talk is saying 'What a strange thing – surely people don't talk to themselves or do they?' you may need to re-read the last paragraph to check which words and meaning you missed. The self-talk has blocked your sensing of the external event. The tonality and volume of your self-talk can also affect state. A sleepy internal voice saying, 'I'm tired' will create weariness. A voice saying, 'I'm energetic and I will do this' may bring you to life.

THE LEADER'S BEHAVIOUR

The final piece is the leader's behaviour that is the outcome of the interplay between self-talk, state, internal representation, and physiology. This behaviour is seen in the external world and influences a response from the external world which is then sensed – and the cycles of behaviour affecting behaviour begins.

The cycles are often reinforcing. If the external event starts positively, with the leader's communication indicating that the follower can complete the task, the follower will pick up on the many cues given – words, body actions, and voice tone. The follower is likely to give a more positive response, and is more likely to generate the behaviours that will create a positive response in the leader. The leader has created a virtuous circle.

On the other hand you could begin by saying, 'I'm not too sure if you can do this' with a hesitant voice tone, down beat tones, and you will get a more negative response – you may have created a debilitating circle leading to lower performance. The leader needs to use all three elements of communication – remembered as the verse (words), the song (tonality) and dance (body) of communication.

Claudia the CEO did not receive the positive response she expected to her declaration of the mission statement. You can explore possible flaws through analysis using the leadership communication model. Key points are:

- The use of PowerPoint and words appeals to the visual and auditory. There was little kinesthetic component.

- Claudia may not have been congruent in her presentation. It is possible that her state, and thus her behaviour, was affected by the late night in preparation of the presentation. Her tiredness and nervousness may have shone through.

- Her message may have been filtered differently by staff. Some staff see 'challenge' as very threatening while others find it 'a great opportunity'. Some were looking for what is good. Some looked for what is bad about her statements. They have different patterns of thinking.

- Some staff perceive their previous experience and memory on initiatives that have not been supported and judge as a generalization that this one will also fail.

Communication is complex, as complex as each individual with whom you communicate. You need to be aware, as is stated in another presupposition of leadership that 'the meaning of any communication is the response you get'. If you are aware of this presupposition you will accept that your communication has not failed, rather you have some feedback where the receiver has interpreted the meaning differently, and you will then, in the nature of the communication cycle, do something differently to get the message over. The key is that you remain aware of others' communication, and that you listen to what they express and the way this is done.

WISDOM FOR LEADERS

■ There go the people. I must follow them for I am their leader.

Prime Minister Balfour

Leaders learn what matters to followers by extending their perceptual position away from the natural first position.

◐ First position (I): You experience the world as it affects you. In this state you fully associate with your experience.

- Second position (you): You process the experience as if you were the follower. You see, hear and feel the experience as the follower.

- Third position (they): You view the experience as you would view a movie from the projection box or as a fly on the wall. In this dissociated state you become detached and take the emotion out of the scene you are watching that involves you.

Gandhi used second position as he prepared to negotiate with civil servants of the British Raj. He associated with the body positions of his adversaries as he moved around the room. Great actors, Meryl Streep and Dustin Hoffman, associate into the beliefs, values and thinking of their characters. They second position their characters.

You may get stuck in one position. People who stay in:

- First position become egotistical.

- Second position become a rescuer, a caretaker.

- Third position become cold and unfeeling.

Discussions with the Australian Ballet's artistic director David McCallister reveal how he uses positioning to great effect: in 'first' to experience what he passionately wants for the company; in 'second' what the needs of the dancers are; and in 'third' what the performance will look like from the audience's perspective.

CHAPTER 7
Unlocking Patterns of Thinking

There are no bastards only meta-programs.

PILAR GODINO

We must have strong minds, ready to accept facts as they are.

HARRY S. TRUMAN

Honest differences are often a healthy sign of progress.

MAHATMA GANDHI

PATTERNS OF THINKING

Ask people to talk about what matters to them, not to ask them to support what matters to us.

Block, *Stewardship*

Powerful filters of how you experience the world are the patterns of thinking, the *meta program*s that you use. Meta programs are sorting filters. They cause you to put your attention in certain places and not in others. You then develop a habitual pattern in how you think, make decisions and behave.

Some people have lots of detail and this detail helps them understand how everything works and fits together and to know exactly what will happen. If detail is your preference, the next paragraph will match how you think and filter.

In this section you will discuss five meta programs. Examples of the two opposites on the meta program continuum will be given, with definitions, examples of the behaviours used by each of the two opposites, and suggestions about how you may communicate effectively to people with each preference. You will then apply the program within a case study and be given a technique to change your pattern if you choose.

An alternative approach using the opposite of detail is to give a big picture. At the end of this section you will understand how you can use meta programs to lead and influence more effectively.

What you 'think' about issues provides your motivation to act. If you 'think' detail your actions will focus on the detail of the issue. If you 'think' big picture your actions will focus on how the issue fits with the strategic environment. When you say, 'He doesn't think like me' it is because he acts differently and when you say, 'She thinks like me', she acts in the same way as you.

Two high technology companies, Worldview and Hitech, have merged to form WorldviewTech. The Managing Director, Elaine, had spent considerable time thinking about the introductory message to all staff. As you read this statement, you may wish to note what parts of the message have had an impact on you and what parts you do not like.

With our stockholder's approval and the closing of our merger, WorldviewTech is positioned to realize the full potential of our enhanced scale and global market presence.

WorldviewTech product line and extensive engineering resources are second to none in the industry. Our expanded customer support capabilities and world class system level expertise will enable us to offer unmatched individualized market support.

All of us at WorldviewTech are thrilled with the rapid successful completion of our merger and feel you have today taken a significant step towards fulfilling our vision of becoming the world's premier network systems provider.

Our company applies the industry's largest history in network systems research and development, as well as over 12 years' field experience to offer unparalleled customer support.

Elaine had asked some staff members for feedback, and the comments had been paradoxical. She had used *perceptual positions* and the *leadership communication model* to help her in her design of the presentation. She was puzzled at some of the negative comments, as she thought she had covered all of the concerns of her staff. The comments are contained within the discussion of the five patterns.

BIG PICTURE–DETAIL
Big picture

Safraz: 'It was difficult to make sense of what was being said. The purpose of the merger wasn't made clear.'

Big picture thinkers:

- Are generally convinced by the overall concept. They may miss the detail required
- Concentrate on leading the overall direction of the project/task
- Respond to the big picture first, and then think of the details and specific pieces
- Tend to summarize tasks and events.

Tell-tale signs:

- They talk about vision, concepts and strategy
- They connect one idea to another different idea
- If they get too much detail they will often ask you to come to the point.

How to communicate with big picture people:

- 🔃 Present the big idea first. Limit the details
- 🔃 Remember they may fill in the detail of your big idea differently
- 🔃 Words to use: overall, framework, idea, flexible.

On the other hand, Safraz was very satisfied with these statements: 'realize the full potential of our enhanced scale and global market presence' and 'becoming the world's premier network systems provider'.

Detail

Jim: 'There wasn't enough detail to understand the mission statement, and you seemed to jump about from strategy to detail back to strategy without getting to grips with the key points and how can you possibly offer "unmatched individualized support"? That would require a lot of detailed planning.'

Detail thinkers:

- 🔃 Break tasks into its parts, often quite small steps
- 🔃 Focus on detail. The details are needed first, and are required before any decision is made
- 🔃 Require concrete examples. Sometimes they lose the overall purpose of the task, as they are lost in the detail.

Tell-tale signs:

🔃 They talk about 'stages, steps, levels' in a task

🔃 When their train of thought is broken, they go back to the start.

How to communicate with 'detail' thinkers:

🔃 Break decisions into parts, and present them in an ordered fashion

🔃 Be specific – ambiguity distracts and confuses them

🔃 Key words: exact, ordered, first, second, third, schedule, breakdown.

Jim was clearly unhappy with the detail that was needed. To appeal to Jim, Elaine would have needed to give the detail on how the company was to supply 'unmatched individualized support'. Until Jim has his level of detail met it is unlikely he will fully buy into the pattern. To appeal to Jim she should say 'We will plan in detail to provide customer support. The first stage will be a Customer Needs Analysis, the second will be . . .'

How do you use both in a presentation?

> If you talk to a man in a language he understands, that goes to his head. If you talk to him in his language, that goes to his heart.

Nelson Mandela (141)

Big Picture–Detail is one of the most important patterns of thinking that you will consider. You will be thinking (at big picture or detail) how may I present input using different patterns? If the presentation is split 50/50 does this mean that 50 per cent of what is said irritates the non-considered thinking pattern? Not really, as the followers are unable to consciously process all of the speech and what they pay attention to is likely to be in their preferred pattern. They delete the bits they don't like! If you included both of Elaine's new statements in a presentation, she would have appealed to both preferences, and she may have received comments such as:

Safraz: 'Great vision. I know where we're going. Something will happen about detailed roll out – it's good I'm sure, and I didn't really catch it' (from the big picture thinker who doesn't want the detail anyway).

Jim: 'Excellent that we'll consider the objective of providing customer support at each level and each stage. It all seemed a bit too inspirational and vague and I know when it's broken down it will make sense' (from the detail thinker).

The key is that you are aware of differing needs and show the flexibility required to meet all needs. You may not be able to meet all needs within one presentation, but when you take questions, be conscious of the thinking pattern of the questioner which you can spot through the tell-tale signs — and answer the questions in their style.

How you are viewed by others

You will have a stronger thinking preference and will find it more comfortable to use your stronger preference. You have varying strengths of preference. You are not one or the other. You have developed this practice since birth and will have at least 20 years of serious practice. And if you have a strong preference it's likely that you will be excellent at using it.

How you are initially perceived by someone depends on both's strength and preference. If you are strongly big picture, most may see you as big picture. Someone who is even more strongly big picture may view you as detail.

EXTERNALLY REFERENCED AND INTERNALLY REFERENCED

This thinking pattern concerns how you judge and decide if something is good or not. The external/internal refers to where you locate your judgement – and how you use it as a reference. Externally referenced people evaluate on the basis of what others think. In contrast, internally referenced people make the decision based on what they think. Churchill was extremely self-referenced as shown in his stance on opposition to Nazi Germany before the Second World War. He knew he was right though few agreed with him at that time. There is a downside to Churchill's strong self-referenced thinking pattern. When things were going badly in Gallipoli during the First World War, he did not seek advice from others because he felt he was right. As a consequence thousands of British and Australian troops were lost.

Margaret Thatcher was strongly internally referenced. When the countries in the Commonwealth were negotiating whether to impose sanctions on South Africa during its Apartheid period, the vote was 49 to one in favour of sanctions. The one vote was cast by the United Kingdom, and significantly by Margaret

Thatcher. When the vote was announced, Thatcher declared, 'I feel sorry for the other forty-nine.'

Internally referenced

Judy: 'I am not impressed by the plans. The merger hasn't been successful in my view, and creating large R and D groups doesn't work.'

Internally referenced thinkers:

- Use their own feelings to know if they have done a good job
- Will not be convinced if they believe they have not met their own target
- Rely on their own views to make decisions
- Are convinced when you appeal to things they already know through their own experiences.

Tell-tale signs:

- They tell us firmly when they decide
- They say, 'I decide', 'I just know'. Feedback from others doesn't tell them when they have done a good job
- They resist when someone else attempts to tell them what's happening.

How to communicate with internally referenced thinkers:

🖎   Ask them what they think. Avoid telling them what others feel about the situation

🖎   Help them to identify their own thinking

🖎   Support an alternative, but say that 'only you will know how to complete this task'. This keeps the notion of choice within themselves and thus they are more likely to consider your proposal as it remains in their control.

To convince Judy, Elaine would have to provide her with the information she needs to make up her own mind. Within the presentation she could say to Judy and others, 'You can ask yourself if you have enough information to make your own mind up', which will move them towards a decision.

Externally referenced

Susan: 'They make all these grand claims but where's the industry benchmark reports that show our products are "second to none"?'

Externally referenced thinkers:

🖎   Require direction from others, and rely on others' views and opinions

- ⟲ Draw conclusions based on others' views
- ⟲ Let others make decisions on how to do it
- ⟲ Conform to others' beliefs
- ⟲ Constantly want to know what others think.

Tell-tale signs:

- ⟲ They ask for lots of feedback on how well things went
- ⟲ They say, 'The facts speak for themselves', 'They told me this was a good idea', 'This is the way it is'
- ⟲ They may describe incoming external information as a decision.

How to communicate with externally referenced thinkers:

- ⟲ Emphasize what other people think, especially authority figures
- ⟲ Give lots of external data such as statistics
- ⟲ Emphasize often 'other people think'.

To convince Susan, Elaine would need to offer industry and internal evidence of benchmarking against world class practice.

OPTIONS AND PROCEDURES THINKERS

Options thinkers

Simone: 'The statement is OK but seems quite restrictive. Yes it's good to provide unmatched support but there are lots of ways of providing support that aren't mentioned, and certainly we can offer products other than network systems.'

Option thinkers are:

- Excited by possibilities, what might be, desire to learn and like to expand options
- Curious about the unknown and what may develop
- Good at developing new procedures and once implemented will consider changing them even though they may be working well.

Tell-tale signs:

- They use lots of words such as 'choose', 'hope', and 'wish'
- They talk about expanding options and exploration of the unknown
- They use action-oriented verbs – 'I will complete this task and get results'
- They say, 'Let's do something different this time.'

How to communicate with options thinkers:

🔃 Provide them with choices in how to implement. Asking them to follow a procedure will cause them difficulty

🔃 Emphasize choices in task completion

🔃 Use words such as 'possibilities', 'choices', 'new ways' and 'alternatives'.

Simone, the options thinker, would find the following statement appealing: 'The new merger provides us with many alternatives in how we carry forward the business. Each business unit will be able to create their own world in whatever way they choose to live out our new vision.'

Procedures thinkers

Michael: 'The difficulty with this presentation is that it's not clear how we are to proceed. There were too many loose ends.'

Procedures thinkers:

🔃 Are motivated by 'need', 'obligation' and necessity – to do something because they must, rather than because they want to

🔃 Want to know the 'right' way to do something

🔃 Have a tendency to accept what comes rather than seek that which is possible and to stay with what is known and secure.

Tell-tale signs:

🔁 They use words such as 'have to', 'must', 'ought to', 'should', 'always'

🔁 They don't talk about options but give the impression that they have to or are obliged to do things and that there isn't a choice. Choice and change may unsettle them

🔁 They like to know in advance what will happen and then stick to it.

How to communicate with procedures thinkers:

🔁 Emphasize the procedures – lay them out step by step, and keep them informed of the steps

🔁 Tell them it's always been done this way when helping them to understand. Even when you are asked for different ways, indicate (as there is in some organizations) there is a procedure for being creative

🔁 Use words such as 'procedure', 'proven ways', 'correct way', 'known way' and 'appropriate'.

Michael will be attracted to this statement: 'There are choices available for each business unit but we have a proven and successful procedure for choosing the correct way. Each business unit will use the Edward de Bono "thinking hats" procedure to generate their business plans.'

SIMILARITY AND DIFFERENCE

Before reading on look at the shapes below and describe the relationship between them. How you describe the relationship gives evidence of your preferred patterns.

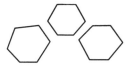

What do you see?

Similarity thinkers

Dorothy: 'The vision is so new and different. It makes me feel uncomfortable as does working with these new people from Technica.'

If you noticed that the shapes were similar and nothing else you have a preference for similarity.

Similarity thinkers:

Tend to look for what's there as opposed to what's missing and match what you are saying with what they already know

🔯 Generalize too quickly based on a few examples, especially when they are alike: 'Ah, that's the same problem. We had a similar problem with two other suppliers.'

Tell-tale signs:

🔯 They use words such as 'same', 'similar', 'in common', 'maintains', 'keep the same'

🔯 They will tell you how a set of objects or situations are similar.

How to *communicate* with similarity thinkers:

🔯 Emphasize areas of mutual agreement

🔯 Discuss familiarity with current and previous situations

🔯 Focus on mutual objectives

🔯 Use words such as 'similar', 'in common', 'maintain', 'keep the same'.

You need to emphasize the similarity with the past, and help Dorothy to focus on what is the same: 'Our focus is as it has always been. Our common themes have been: customer service and responses to customers. We will maintain our standards, and then gradually increase them, as we have in the past.'

Difference thinkers

Maire: 'There's nothing new in the initiative. It's not worthwhile.'

If you looked at the hexagons diagram and noticed one was higher, lower, left, right, you are likely to run differences. People who use this pattern notice what is different – and often disagree with your view immediately. People who do this consistently are called *mismatchers*. If you say something is black, their immediate response will be it could be white. McNish, the carpenter in Shackleton, was a mismatcher. When Shackleton told him something was 'impossible' he said, 'No, it's not. I can do it.'

Difference thinkers:

- ↻ Tend to search for what's missing

- ↻ Will mismatch as a way to understanding. They naturally make the opposite point so they can understand. You may interpret this response as persistent and unnecessary objecting. You may even say they are 'awkward', 'bloody-minded', or 'twisted'. Remember *behaviour is not identity* – they are using their preferred pattern – mismatching!

ⓝ Will notice how things don't fit together.

Tell-tale signs:

ⓝ They use phrases like 'day and night', 'no relationship', 'no comparison'

ⓝ You will hear the phrase 'yes, but' a lot

ⓝ They discuss how 'things have changed'

ⓝ They use words such as 'new', 'changed', 'radical', and 'revolutionary'.

How to communicate with difference thinkers:

ⓝ Emphasize the differences

ⓝ Present ideas in the frame of being very different

ⓝ Use their 'tell tale' words.

Maire would be comfortable with a response such as: 'While our vision remains the same as it was in Hitech and Worldview [we have just said this to appeal to the Similarity thinkers] there is much that is more radical thinking; we will redesign our customer care to be even more customer focused . . .'

MOVING AWAY FROM—MOVING TOWARDS
Moving away

Joshua: 'It's another crazy push forwards. I bet they haven't thought of how we'll increase the sales force to cope with the new business, or how we are going to produce all the new products, let alone the changes that will be required in my department. At least they have acknowledged our history in network systems, and 12 years' experience in customer support. Nonetheless this change is dangerous.'

Away from thinkers:

- Focus on negative consequences and may be overly distracted by them.

- Move away from problems they don't want or like

- Often have trouble defining what they **do** want and can have difficulty with goals

Tell-tale signs:

- They talk about what they don't want, and what they don't want to happen

- They tell you what they will 'avoid', 'stay away from' and 'get out of'.

How to communicate with 'away from' thinkers:

- Find out what they don't want, and empathize that you can help them avoid it
- Anticipate problems, and reassure them the problem can be solved
- Be patient with their potential inability to tell you what they want.

Joshua would be reassured by the response: 'I understand there are issues with merging departments and providing the best customer support. We will build on what we have done successfully before, use the experience we have in dealing with change, and plan to provide the resources to support the inevitable problems of change.'

Moving towards

Ali was pleased with the statement. He could envisage the successful merger and that it would contribute to the vision.

People who move towards:

- Move towards what they want
- Often have difficulty in recognizing what should be avoided
- Often minimize negative consequences, or are even oblivious to what is not working as they work in pursuit of their goal.

Tell-tale signs:

- ⓑ They talk about what they want
- ⓑ They talk about people and things they want to include
- ⓑ They use words like 'attain', 'gain', 'accomplish', 'obtain', 'achieve'.

Communicating with 'moving towards' people:

- ⓑ Focus on the stated goals and what they want to achieve
- ⓑ Emphasize that what you are doing will help them to get what they want.

It is likely that you will run both patterns with a primary motivation and a secondary follow up. You may be motivated towards, and check on what can go wrong, or you may consider first what you wish to avoid, and then move towards what you wish to achieve.

Entrepreneurs, both inside and outside an organization, tend to be towards. They go for goals and often don't fully consider the downside. Lawyers and safety experts use mostly away from patterns, helping you avoid unpleasant consequences. The clash between the patterns can be interesting – 'I just want to close this deal' (the towards person), but what if A happens, and B . . . and Z' (the away from person) – and as we need to remind ourselves, both approaches are just different thinking patterns that result in different behaviours.

MORE PATTERNS

You have explored five of the key patterns of thinking. As people are complex, you will not be surprised that many more patterns have been identified. You will, for example, observe people who are proactive compared to reactive. Other patterns are discussed in the books of Charvet, Hall and Bodenhamer listed in the Further Reading section at the end of this chapter.

HOW YOU CAN CHANGE YOUR PATTERN OF THINKING

The focus of this chapter is about communicating with others and as you read about the patterns of thinking you may have identified patterns you use that are not useful. For example, you may have recognized that in your desire to reach goals (the *towards* pattern) you have ignored some key issues that might stop you (the *away froms*). In working with the Managing Director of a fast-growing company and discussing yet more acquisitions, the authors asked him, 'What happens if you become seriously ill?' The response was, 'I won't and we'll still get there.' Eventually 'key person' insurance was bought to cover the potential illness, an away from. If he ran 'away from' it would have been purchased years ago – as also would the pension, and other life assurance products.

Alternatively you may be able to articulate well what you didn't want but not what you do. It can be said of political parties in opposition that often they know what they don't want (the ruling party's policy) but they don't know what they do want.

Progress now

Change your pattern of thinking

Your pattern of thinking can be stretched and adjusted. Since the patterns inform the brain about what to sort and delete, if, for example, you move towards you delete or pay less attention to what you move away from and if you move away from you delete or pay less attention to what you move towards. If you direct your conscious thoughts to the deleted part you can access more resource and choice in your behaviour. The stages are:

1   Identify the pattern that currently does not serve you well and undermines your effectiveness.

2   Describe the thinking pattern you wish to use more readily. Indicate why, where, and when you wish to use it.

3   Try it out in your head. Say the words that will be unfamiliar, think the pattern that is different. If you know someone who runs the pattern you would like, put yourself in that second position you discussed in Chapter 6 – and see, feel and hear what they would do.

4   Check that you really want to change the pattern in the context you are thinking of. You have learned it well over the years, and it has had a

positive intention for you! Decide if the new behaviour is how you want to be. How will the new behaviour, and use of a different pattern, affect you and others around you?

5   If you have satisfactory answers to the above, 'install' the new pattern. Give yourself permission to use it. You are, after all, *in charge of your own brain*! You may find that your self-talk will point out a difficulty. If you decided to use towards, a voice from your past, parent/professional adviser, might say, 'Be careful, if you don't think about what might go wrong you'll lose everything, so don't do it.' Listen to these concerns and answer them. Say to the voice, 'I will be careful, I will consider all the stages, and the loss is of such a value – so I can't lose everything.'

6   Think of how the pattern will work in the future – and use it until it becomes comfortable.

And you have permission to change back!

Further reading

Charvet, Shelle Rose, 1997, *Words that Change Minds: Mastering the Language of Influence* (2nd edition), Dubuque, Iowa: Kendall/Hunt.

Hall, Michael and Bodenhamer, Bob, 1997, *Design Engineering with Meta-Programs*, Carmarthen, Wales: Crown Publishing.

CHAPTER 8
Communicating Powerfully

If you can dream it, you can do it.

WALT DISNEY

Everything should be made as simple as possible, but not simpler.

ALBERT EINSTEIN

USING LANGUAGE

As a leader you will want to communicate powerfully with your followers. You want to be able to determine precisely what a person means by the words he or she uses. The use of language can give your follower a different way of thinking about something that gives it another meaning for them – and that other meaning can give them choices. In doing so you get the more precise view of their 'map'. *Precision questioning* gives you these skills. At other times you can communicate powerfully by using artfully vague language such that the follower can access thoughts and resources that may be hidden. With more resources they can be more flexible in their actions. How you help followers to connect with these resources is the role of *fuzzy language* and the words you use can make people feel powerless to act. We suggest that you cease to use the three words – *can't, try, but* – that disempower.

Progress now

You will need to involve two or three others in this exercise. Write down five words that mean entertainment to you. Ask two other people to complete the same task. Now compare the lists.

You may find some commonality and much difference. When we completed this exercise with our colleagues Sean stated entertainment to be 'fun, company, enjoyment, music and frivolity'. Anne said it was 'TV, cinema, theatre, musicals and videos'. In this instance our colleague chose to describe the how of entertainment rather than the what. A third colleague, Mavis had 'fun, conversation, dining out and skiing' on her list, a mixture of what and how. We asked her 'what specifically do you mean by fun?' She said 'going shopping with my girlfriends'. Sean, when asked 'what is fun?' said 'playing golf with my colleagues'. Note the difference. Yet everyone knows what fun is! If you have not completed the exercise it will make sense that we have different meanings for words and the meaning is only about an intellectual level. Remember the time you said to your partner, 'let's have an entertaining weekend' – and they designed the weekend from hell – for you! So there is no commonality on the meaning of entertainment.

BACKGROUND TO PRECISION LANGUAGE

You are going to consider 12 questioning patterns that will allow you to get to the meaning of a communication with a person. To help you understand the questioning process it is useful to understand the difference between the *surface* and *deep structure of language*.

Surface structure is represented by the words or sentences that you speak. Deep structure is the *internal representation*, the experience of what you seek to communicate. Deep structure is what you really want to say but it is not conscious. If you used deep structure to communicate you would become very long winded – so what you do is *delete*, *distort* and *generalize*, as discussed in Chapter 6. The message becomes the shorter but less precise message at surface level.

Using *precision language* you seek to unravel the generalizations, deletions and distortions that others use and get to their deep structure to their 'map' of the world. If you do this you can begin to communicate within their map. Otherwise you may speak at cross-purposes, with subsequent confusion.

A company asked for a review of their communications strategy. They were committed to open and direct communication. The report from the consultants contained quotations from the staff members that appeared to raise more questions than answers. The Director of Communications, Asif, wanted to get finer detail in order to plan the necessary changes. He wanted to get the level of information required at a deep structure level. The phrases that he wanted to dig deeper into were:

'They don't listen to me in this organization.'

'I feel as if I am being manipulated.'

'Communication is better in the sales department.'

'My supervisor handled the communication meeting badly.'

'It's clear that we need to improve how we present our message.'

'What is required is more honesty and respect in our communication.'

'I can't make sense of what is being said.'

'We must provide an in-company newsletter. Everyone issues an in-company newsletter.'

'I know that all the managers are worried about communication.'

> 'Communication will never work here, until senior managers are more open.'

> 'When we get the IT system in place, we will be able to improve communication.'

> 'Because the senior managers won't talk directly to us, they don't want to tell us what's happening.'

The Director of Communication knew who had made each statement, and chose to go back to interview each person again.

HOW TO USE PRECISION LANGUAGE

To take you through how to get more precise information about surface statements each phrase will be discussed and you will be shown how to use precision language to move from *surface* to *deep structure*. Twelve categories of precision question are discussed.

Unspecified nouns

'**They** don't listen to me in this organization.'

In this case Asif doesn't know who 'they' are. It could be co-workers, supervisors, managers or any other group. Unspecified nouns are clarified by using the question, 'Who (or what) specifically?'

Unspecified verbs

'I feel as if I am being **manipulated**.'

The verb 'manipulate' is vague and non-specific. Manipulate describes an action or process but so much information is deleted that you cannot have a clear representation of the meaning of the action. Was it that the person behaved against their will, or was stopped from doing something, or just felt bad? If you need more detail on the manipulation you need to ask, 'How specifically did . . . ?'

Comparison

'Communication is **better** in the sales department.'

'My supervisors handled our communication meeting **badly**.'

In the first statement communication is being compared to other departments through the use of 'better'. But you need to know better than what: Better than it was before? Better than another department? When you use 'best', 'better', 'worse', or 'worst' you are making a comparison. You can only make a comparison when you know compared to what.

In the second statement the judgement is made that the supervisor handles communication meetings 'badly'. 'Badly' compared to what? How the person who made the statement would have done it? How his manager would have handled it?

Often the deleted part of the comparison is unrealistic. If someone had said to you 'You handled that presentation badly' and had deleted the comparison (compared to a brilliant presenter) you are left with a feeling of inadequacy. And you may then believe there is nothing you can do about improving your presentation skills.

If you wish to clarify a comparison you ask, 'Compared with what, whom . . . ?'

Judgement

'**It's clear** that we need to improve how we present our message.'

This statement raises the question 'clear to whom?'. The management team, the individual, the whole company? And on what grounds is it clear? Where is the evidence that makes it clear? Do we have customer feedback, a survey completed, or is it one person's view?' To clarify the judgements you need to ask: 'Who is making the judgement, and what evidence do they have for making it?'

Actions into nouns

'What is required is more **honesty** and **respect** in our **communication**.'

In the statement above there are three verbs turned into nouns – honesty, respect and communication. Each needs to be explored to recover the process and action. To discover more meaning you need to ask 'How would you know they were honest?'. You need to ask 'Who's not communicating?', 'How would you like to communicate?', 'How should others communicate?'. With 'respect' you need to ask, 'Who is respecting whom and how are they doing it?'

Language of possibility

'I **can't** make sense of what is being said.'

The person who made this statement has defined that they can't (ever) make sense of the statements. If they remain of this viewpoint they will continue not to be able to make sense of it. Most people can, if they want to make the effort, make sense of something. It may be that the person is choosing not to make sense — for many reasons that are contained in their experience, memories, belief and values. The 'I can't' becomes an absolute state, not amenable to change.

The language of possibility contains words such as: can/can't; possible/impossible; will/won't; and may/may not. The questions that get clarification are: 'What stops you from . . . ?', 'What would happen if you did . . . ?'

Language of necessity

'We **must** provide an in-company newsletter.'

Implied in this statement is a rule of conduct that is not explicit. You have no idea for the basis for the rule. If you take action and implement the newsletter you may miss other opportunities for reaching the implied goal, better communications. The use of 'must' and 'should' when you talk to someone often implies failure in the other person. A feeling of guilt that they should be able to do the task is installed.

Clarification on 'must/must not', 'should/shouldn't', 'have to', 'need to', 'and it is necessary to' is achieved by asking: 'What would happen if you did/didn't . . . ?', 'Or?'.

Generalization

'**Everyone** issues an in-company newsletter.'

Generalization is a very common form of imprecise language. A limited experience is taken to apply to an entire category. The person who said this has experience of companies that have newsletters and has generalized to all companies.

You can spot generalizations by the words 'every', 'all', 'never', 'no one'. Sometimes the generalization is implied as in 'email messages are the key to effective communication'. The person who states this has not been faced with, or does not remember, the 150 new mail messages that have arrived – many of which are of no use. Challenges to generalizations that flush out the exceptions are to bounce back the generalization as a challenging question: 'All . . . ?', 'Never . . . ?' and 'Has there ever been a time when . . . ?'

Mind reading

'**I know** all the managers are worried about communication.'

This statement appears to be a significant endorsement of the need for the investment in the new communications system. The manager may have thought about communication and she may well be worried — she is assuming, without any evidence, that others share her concerns. If this manager was talking to other managers and said, 'I know you all are worried about communication', she may set up a self-fulfilling cycle where they begin to believe they should be worried, and begin to be! Challenge to the mind-reader is: 'How exactly do you know . . . ?'

Cause and effect

'Communications will never work here, **until** senior managers **are more open**.'

In this statement the problem is 'communications' and the course has been shifted to the senior managers. If they are more open then communication will work better. This form of distortion puts the individual who stated this at the control of senior managers. It may be true that senior managers need to be more open – and there are also actions that this manager could take to improve communications.

Challenges to cause and effect are: 'How specifically does . . . cause . . . ?'

Presuppositions

'When we get the IT system in place, we will be able to improve communication.'

This statement incorporates previous beliefs and *expectations* that presuppose 'if the IT system is in place' communication will be improved. It may be necessary to challenge this basic assumption as it limits choice. Communication can be improved by other means – the initial challenge to the *presupposition* is: 'What makes you believe that . . . ?'

Complex relationship

'Because the senior managers won't talk directly to us, they don't want to tell us what is happening.'

There is some mind reading in this statement on the links between the two parts of the statements. Senior managers may wish to cascade communication down through the organization and do not choose to do so, as they wish the immediate manager to undertake the task. There is no evidence that because 'senior managers won't talk directly to us' that 'they don't want to tell us what is happening'.

The question to find out more about the complex relationship is: 'How does x mean y?'

Conclusion

You have considered twelve patterns that allow us to probe into the deep structure of someone's map to get a richer and fuller understanding of their world. In doing so you explore further the three map-making processes of generalization, deletion and distortion. You can also use the same questioning on your own self-talk. The next time you say 'I can't', (a language of possibility) ask yourself 'What's stopping me?'

Progress now

In reality a sentence may often contain more than one example of imprecise language. Identify the pattern within this sentence and compare with the given correct answer.

'Why don't the incompetent directors stop trying to communicate with me? It always just annoys me. I know I should remain calmer but I can't.'

Answer

This sentence contains mind reading and presuppositions (the directors are trying to annoy me), cause and effect (communication annoys me), generalization (always), judgement (incompetent), comparison (calmer), language of possibility (can't), language of necessity (should), unspecified verbs (trying), actions into nouns (calm), and unspecified nouns (IT, directors).

BENEFITS OF PRECISION QUESTIONING

Exploring the deep structure of meaning using precision language is very powerful as it:

🜋 Allows you to gather the high quality data so you understand what people mean

🜋 Provides clarity of meaning so you know exactly what the other person means

🜋 Gives you choices: generalization, actions with nouns, and presuppositions all set limits – and the limits exist in the word, not in the world. If you believe 'no one can achieve that' (a generalization), the words provide a limit to your actions.

Our experience is that it is often the less powerful precision questions that are overused. At leadership training we often hear over the dinner table, 'What specifically do you mean by entertainment?' Possibly amusing at first, it can begin to irritate the speaker as the imprecision in every sentence is exposed, and the flow of communication is interrupted. You move quickly towards a, 'Stop doing that'. You may move towards precision and the critical potential loss of rapport. So be cautious of overusing precision questions and remember if you break rapport, all the precise information in the world will not allow you to get the information you want and to influence the follower.

Progress now

You have considered twelve precision patterns and the precision questions that provide more in-depth data. The table below shows the pattern in summary.

Pattern	Precision question
Unspecified noun	Who (or what) specifically?
Unspecified verbs	How specifically did?

Pattern	Precision question
Comparison	Compared with what, when?
Performer	Who is making the judgement?
Actions into nouns	Who is . . . and how are they doing it?
Language of possibility	What stops you?
Language of necessity	What would happen if?
Generalization	Everyone?
Mind reading	How exactly do you know?
Cause and effect	How specifically does . . . cause . . . ?
Complex relationship	How does . . . mean?
Presupposition	What makes you believe?

Now photocopy the table, and put it into your pocket, organizer, or have a copy available at meetings. Pick one pattern for each of the next twelve days and listen for its use. If useful, challenge the pattern. You will find that you will soon have the model in your unconscious and it is a resource that is available to use. Be cautious of misuse and losing rapport.

'FUZZY' LANGUAGE TO CREATE MEANING

That's a great deal to make one word mean,' Alice said in a thoughtful tone.

'When I make a word do a lot of work like that,' said Humpty Dumpty, 'I always pay extra.'

Lewis Carroll, *Alice Through the Looking Glass*

Precision language allows you to get to the deeper meaning that people have in their heads. Now you can learn 'fuzzy' language, to allow followers to create their own 'new world' to which they wish to belong. In doing so you may win their hearts and minds because you will engage their emotions and increase rapport with them.

With fuzzy language you deliberately choose to use unspecified verbs and nouns that allow the listener to make their own interpretation in their 'world' to positively create their own generalizations, distortion and deletion. This technique is the opposite of precision questioning which is useful to drill down to the meaning at a deeper level. An inspirational speech will use 'fuzzy' language to allow the individual to create meaning. For example in his inaugural speech in 1963, John F. Kennedy stated: 'And so, my fellow Americans, ask not what your country can do for you, ask what you can do for your country.' The follower can choose what they wish to 'do', and there is ambiguity in what is 'your country'.

You will probably recognize this skilful use of language in many modern advertising slogans. A proponent of artfully vague language patterns was Milton Erickson, a psychotherapist who was an expert creator of trance conditions that allowed, in his case, clients to access their internal resources. A key part of his technique was to build rapport with clients so they would be open to his suggestions of new resources.

This technique can be applied in your leadership. When you use fuzzy language artfully, the follower must fill in the details and actively search for the meaning of what is heard from *their own experience*, and in doing so, allow you to connect with their experience. In the following example, Sian is making a presentation to a mixed audience with different values, beliefs and views and she wishes to appeal to all. The following description shows how Sian has skilfully used the technique of fuzzy language. You will also see that she uses the influencing technique of match–pace–lead:

Match with the Yes set

Create the conditions in which the followers are saying 'yes, yes, yes', which creates a positive direction with them. This is a common part of influencing where you want to get the follower to say 'yes'. As Sian says:

'Hi, I'm Sian O'Hara. We are here today [*yes*] after the planning work that has gone on in the last months [*yes*]. Some of you will want to have the broad picture and some the final detail [the choice of two means mismatchers (discussed in Chapter 7) will have to say *yes* to one!]. You will now be interested in the financial plan.'

Pace

Pacing is critical to building rapport so the audience is receptive to the message. It is likely that the rapport will come from using a metaphor from a common human experience that all can relate to, such as raising a family, going to school, and choosing a group such as accountants or lawyers who have different views. Sian continues:

'The creation of the marketing plan has been like raising a child, and you will recognize the stages in the process as either a parent or child or both. The early years are full of wonderment and first learning, then we get to school and rules are imposed (in our case by the accountants rather than the teachers), and then we go through adolescence – a bit uncertain – and then to maturity where we know we can do it!'

Lead

In this stage you introduce in a fuzzy way the reverse of the patterns from precision language. Doing this allows listeners to value their experience, and sense of what is happening and to lead them towards a positive and exciting internal representation. Sian is moving them forward, allowing her followers to create a world that she wants them to join. Read the speech as one piece and note how the language is fuzzy.

'I know that you are curious and that means you will learn that much better about our success last year. It's a good thing to consider first what happened last year and to base the plan on this experience. We will be able to go forward to greater achievements next year. We must be focused on next year, so what is the plan all about?'

Language	Interpretation
I know that you are curious	*Mindread* that embeds the command that individuals are curious.
and that means you will learn	*Complex relationship* that implies being curious means that you will learn.
that much better about our success last year.	*Comparison* – better than whatever comparison people choose.
It's a good thing to consider first what happened last year	*Judgement* – who says, and the command is that it is a good thing.
and to base the plan on this experience.	*Complex relationship* again – another command that plans should be based on last year.
We will be able to go forward to greater achievement next year.	*Comparison and action in noun* – each person can select their own achievement – and make it better.
We must	*Language of necessity* – really meaning the organization states that.
be focused on next year	*Unspecified verb* – each focus in their own way.

The key to the creation of the artfully vague, fuzzy language is to utilize as opposites all those patterns that you analysed in precision questioning. You do not drill to the deeper meaning; rather, by not being specific, allow the listener to create their own meaning. The other pattern used above was to keep a smooth flow of language – use lots of joining words, such as since, when, if, then, while, became, even, and, so what.

Progress now

Analyse the excerpt of UK Prime Minister Tony Blair's speech after 11 September 2001. First look for the precision language patterns, and the question you would ask to get to the deeper meaning. Then recognize how by **not** answering these questions, Tony Blair creates a rich vision for his followers.

Quote from a speech by Tony Blair to the Labour Party Conference on 2 October 2001. He has introduced 'September 11' attacks on America as a turning point in history and relates an experience he had at a New York church service two weeks previously:

> *I believe their memorial can and should be greater than simply the punishment of the guilty. It is that out of the shadow of this evil, should emerge lasting good: destruction of the machinery of terrorism wherever it is found; hope amongst all nations of a new beginning where we seek to resolve differences in a calm and ordered way; greater understanding between nations and between faiths; and above all justice and prosperity for the poor and dispossessed, so that people everywhere can see the chance of a better future through the hard work and creative power of the free citizen, not the violence and savagery of the fanatic. I know that here in Britain people are anxious, even a little frightened. I understand that. People know we must act but they worry what might follow.*

'*I believe* [a mindread, that it is possible] their memorial *can* [language of possibility – it can happen is the message for the listener] and *should* [language of necessity – it must happen] be greater than simply the *punishment* [unspecified noun – the listeners create their appropriate punishment] of the guilty. It is that out of the shadow of this evil, should emerge lasting good: [a cause and effect – that the shadow will create a lasting good] *destruction* of the machinery of *terrorism* [unspecified nouns – listeners will add their meaning to 'destruction' and 'terrorism']

wherever it is found; hope amongst *all* nations [generalization –
do all nations want this or just nations like us?] of a new
beginning where *we* [lost performer – who are the 'we'?] seek to
resolve differences in a calm and ordered way; greater
understanding [action into noun: that there is such a thing
rather than being a process] between *nations* and between
faiths; [unspecified nouns – which nations and faiths?] and
above all justice and prosperity for the poor and dispossessed,
so that people everywhere [generalization – all people?] can see
the chance of a better future through the hard work and creative
power of the free citizen, [complex relationship: how does 'hard
work and creative power' allow us to 'see the chance of a better
future'?] not the violence and savagery of the fanatic. I know
that *here in Britain people are anxious, even a little frightened*
[presupposition – what makes you believe this is the case?]. I
understand that. People know we must act but they worry what
might follow.'

Artfully vague fuzzy language is at the basis of the power of this
speech. The use of artfully vague language does not imply the
speaker is not genuine. What it does do is to allow listeners to
associate their own experience with the speaker's world.

THREE WORDS THAT STOP

You have seen how language can have a great effect in influencing others. However, there are words that stop people in their tracks and disempower them. They create a negative state within people, and inhibit the organization. The words are 'try', 'can't', and 'but'.

Try

'Try to turn over to the next page.'

Did you? If so you succeeded. Why not say, 'Turn over to the next page'? 'Try' admits the possibility of failure. If you ask followers to 'try' to complete a task by the morning, you have given them the permission to fail. They can reply, 'I tried but was not able to . . .' Replace try with a positive statement such as 'will'. 'Will' forces us to think through whether it is feasible for the person asked to complete the task. If it is not feasible, why ask them? You only open up the possibility of frustration and overload for them. If they have the resolve and time, then use 'will'. 'You will be able to produce that information by tomorrow.' If you replace 'try' with 'will' in your own thoughts, you will be clearer about your commitment to succeed.

Can't

'I can't get anyone to understand'.

'Can't' implies that it is impossible, that you have no further options open to you. If you say, 'I haven't yet got anyone to understand', you leave open the options to find a way to do it. You may also say, 'What would it be like if you could . . .' to unlock possible solutions. Talk about what you can do, rather than can't.

But

'I think you have a good idea, but . . .'

Read the phrase above, then read this phrase: 'I think you have a good idea and . . .'

Compare the difference in how you feel. You may find the first statement makes you feel less positive. 'But' negates the statement that goes before it: The message that is received is, 'You don't have a good idea' and 'I have a much better one', whereas 'and' allows acknowledgement of the idea or an addition to it. Avoid using the soft 'buts' such as 'however':

however gives the same message, that you are deleting the other person's idea.

Progress now

Stop using 'can't', 'but' and 'try'. Note the difference in the response you get, using your awareness.

CHAPTER 9
Interacting as a Leader

Cometh the hour, cometh the man.

ANON

These are the hard times in which a genius would wish to live. Great necessities call forth great leaders.

ABIGAIL ADAMS IN A LETTER TO
THOMAS JEFFERSON, 1790

DEVELOPING THE ROLE OF THE LEADER – THINGS THAT COUNT

Jack Welch, the former CEO at General Electric, said, 'Being comfortable in your own skin is the best gift you can give yourself. . . . It is up to us to define ourselves and what we want to be.' Welch talks about the need for passion. 'Those who care most, win,' he declares. 'It's about getting into the skin of every employee. It is about imparting energy. Work should be fun, a game, something in the soul as well as in the wallet.' This statement shows the importance of people having a positive reason (a *towards* thinking pattern) to do what they are doing.

The people around you will also be pleased to see the real you. Welch states, 'You have to be visible to every constituency. Leadership is about being out there.' Woody Allen said, 'Eighty per cent of success is just showing up.' Taking this thought further, leadership is about being seen in many circumstances and connecting with people in all of them. A leader is less effective if seen only when things are difficult. A cry from front line service workers is often, 'We only see you when there is a problem.' This pattern, if oft repeated, leads to the sighting of 'you' being associated with a problem. This pattern is likely to trigger negative internal thoughts in others and will make it less likely that you can create the positive interaction from others that you desire. On the other hand, a leader who is often seen, in good times and in bad, and remains at ease in both circumstances, is more likely to be admired as a leader.

RESOURCEFUL IN A CRISIS

At the time of the terrorist attacks of 11 September 2001, being seen and being himself was a big part of how **Rudy Giuliani**, New York's Mayor, tackled the events that followed. He was on the scene at once, a reassuring, capable presence. Being there and interacting with people was the vision we all had of him *being* the leader. The way he was seen to talk with and listen to others at the scene gave the impression that these interactions would influence his thinking and actions following the tragedy. Contrast this with the politician who is kept away from the crowds by teams of advisers and shown only what they want to see. One seems connected, the other seems cocooned. Consider the emotions, and feelings that Mayor Giuliani may have had at the time. His mind, like everybody else's, would have been full of uncertainty and shock and yet he would have known that letting those feelings overpower him would not have been what was required. He needed to find his own *resourceful state* to do what he needed to do by letting his qualities shine through and inspire others.

In contrast there is a story from a high-tech company specializing in internet banking transfers that was recently subjected to a hostile takeover by a bank. The bank finally won and there was a high level of anxiety among the staff. The share price had fallen dramatically and many staff were shareholders. They knew the bank would not take everyone on, and the rumour machine had started. The CEO had a meeting with staff where he attempted to reassure them. He commiserated with their loss of share values, and it became apparent that while he had lost money in the deal, overall he would do very nicely through his payouts. The meeting was fraught and afterwards many people wanted to address issues with the CEO. The CEO at this point decided to take a week's leave and instructed his Director of HR to deal with the flack. She did a great job and gained credibility through her connection with people, practical advice and willingness to just listen. He, on the other hand, was described as weak, evasive and cowardly by his staff.

If you want to manage somebody, manage yourself. Do that well and you will be ready to stop managing. And start leading.

Message published in the *Wall St Journal* by United Technologies

HONING AND IMPROVING RELATIONSHIPS

One of the things that may hold back emergent leaders is their fear of failure and what people will say or think about them.

Sir Chay Blythe, leader in round the world sailing, states, 'Intellectual behaviours are still critical for leaders, but relationships are essential for achieving success. Leaders of today need to be able to deal with people, to build, nurture and develop long-term relationships, show sensitivity, flexibility, and be more prepared to help others to learn.'

The relationships you have with others are crucial. In the past you may have thought of these in terms of how you direct their behaviour. Another powerful route to effectiveness is to understand what it is they need from you: what an individual needs more of, or less of, to create the circumstances needed to be fully committed to achieving an agreed outcome, and to be creative in the ways in which it is done.

Creating optimal conditions for generating exceptional and exhilarating performances from others is like turning a key to a powerhouse of talent, creativity and productivity. It makes sense to use it well. A key to creating these optimal conditions is effective feedback.

FEEDBACK: OPENING THE CHANNELS OF COMMUNICATION

Why give and receive feedback?

Feedback is the receipt of information about what you do. In the past you may have referred to it as criticism and then as either positive or negative criticism. You may even have referred to it as failure. But it is more useful to presuppose that *there is no failure, only feedback.*

We may not habitually step forward for feedback, however, it is a great habit to develop. So why is it good to get feedback? At a recent seminar conducted by Q Learning these were the top ten benefits of receiving feedback cited by the leaders in attendance:

1 It will help me to improve.

2 It will save me from repeating unhelpful behaviour.

3 It helps me to become aware of patterns that I run.

4 It is motivating.

5 I can measure change.

6   I know what is expected of me.

7   I know how others perceive me.

8   I can find out what they really want of me.

9   It ultimately saves me time and energy.

10   It will increase my ability to influence others.

These benefits are powerful reasons to give and seek feedback. Unfortunately people may be reluctant to tell you how they feel about something, and the skill of giving high quality feedback is in short supply in many organizations.

How to give quality feedback

Feedback delivered well is empowering. Some important characteristics of quality feedback are explored below.

High quality feedback is best given face to face and when there is rapport. Remember that 93 per cent of communication is delivered through body language (55 per cent) and tone of voice (38 per cent), and only 7 per cent through the words you use.

When you give feedback use specific examples of behaviour. State what you have seen the person do, heard them say or what you have felt in relation to their actions. Talk about the behaviour and don't imply any significance to their identity. 'You were 10 minutes late for work on Tuesday' is an accurate statement. 'You are a lazy, insolent layabout' is not! So what has happened here is that the feedback has moved from behaviour to identity. In this case a concern about a behaviour becomes an attack on identity, so prepare for a vigorous response, such as, 'How dare you. I am a good worker.' The issue of the lateness will not be appropriately addressed as bigger issues have overwhelmed it.

Acknowledge that feedback is from your point of view; it is information about how you perceive things. Check what your intention is in giving feedback. Does it have a positive intention towards the other person, or are you saying something to make yourself feel better?

Feedback is best when it is about things that can be changed; commenting on what cannot be changed is less helpful. Where things can be changed, talk about what you want rather than what you don't want.

Give the opportunity for feedback to be two-way. There may be things you are doing that affect the situation. Clarify and use open questions to obtain specific examples of the behaviour the other person mentions. Be aware of your body language and any gestures you use, together with your voice tone and volume. How would what you are saying be viewed and heard if you were the person on the receiving end? Is this the way you would like to be spoken to?

Feedback should always be timely and as close to the event that has taken place as is appropriate. Use your judgement about the right environment, and how much rapport there is between you. For feedback to be really effective, limit the points you are making to the two or three things that will make the most difference. Any more than this and the recipient is likely either to forget or feel oppressed.

Avoid the word BUT: 'I really liked your presentation but it would be better if you spoke up more as I couldn't hear everything you said.' When the brain hears the word 'but' it often deletes all the meaning that goes before it. In this example the recipient is likely not to have kept in mind that you liked the presentation and simply concentrated on your later remark. Just by changing the 'but' to an 'and' can increase the chances of your feedback being accepted. Re-presenting that sentence, you get, 'I really liked your presentation and it would be even better if you spoke up more as I couldn't hear everything you said.' Use this, and it will work. 'But' is one of the words that stop.

For leaders who have limited experience of giving feedback it is rated as being one of the most stressful management activities. Those who give feedback habitually find it one of their most effective management tools. Anyone giving feedback – even if it is not done perfectly – deserves a pat on the back.

RECEIVING FEEDBACK

> I have six honest serving men; they are How, What, Why, Who, Where and When.
>
> Rudyard Kipling

The golden rules for receiving feedback are: Learn what you can from the feedback you are given, and genuinely listen to what others say. Avoid explaining, justifying, defending or placating. Say 'thank you'. This acknowledges that the message has been received. It also gives you time to evaluate what has been said. All feedback is just data: what you do with it is your choice. And remember, choice is better than no choice. Whatever you do there are consequences, so you can choose what you want to do with the data received. Saying 'thank you' to someone makes him or her feel good and more likely to give you valuable feedback in the future.

When receiving unfavourable feedback, ask 'What would you prefer me to do instead?' This question moves the focus of the discussion to what the individual would like and helps you to understand specific desired behaviour. It helps you to gain an insight into how that person sees you.

Use open questions. Questions that begin with How, What, When, Who, Where and Why.

Link each of these with 'specifically' to gain even more clarity. How specifically would you prefer to have that done? What specifically would you like me to do? – and so on. Remember to manage your tone of voice and body positioning when asking these questions.

Finally, give yourself time to let feedback sink in. Sleep on it. Say, 'I would like to think over what you have said before responding.' A final reminder, finish by saying 'Thank you.'

FEEDBACK TECHNIQUES

There are some helpful techniques to use in structuring feedback you are giving others. These techniques work equally well for feedback for yourself, feedback and review sessions for groups.

More from me – Less from me

How to improve your input into a relationship is a critical skill for a leader. This will be especially true when someone is leading in the style of Individualized Consideration. As Chay Blythe says, to improve your relationship with someone ask them what they need more of from you and what they need less of from you. Here is a method to find out that information. By carrying out the exercise you will elicit a valuable piece of feedback and make a positive impact on achieving a commonly held desirable outcome.

Progress now

1   Consider a person with whom the relationship is not what you, or they, want yet.

2   Agree with them a short-term outcome that both want.

3   State that you want him or her to succeed and recognize that you could change your approach.

4   Ask 'What would you like **more** of from me to achieve this?'

5   Ask them, 'What would you like **less** of from me to achieve this?'

6   Thank them for the feedback and commit to the changes you will make for the timeframe you have agreed in order to achieve the objective.

7   Review effectiveness and the difference your behaviour has made to you, the other person and to the outcome that you set.

Stop, Start, Continue

'Stop, Start, Continue' is a delightfully clean way to give 'pin-pointed' accurate feedback. You need to remember to apply all the other rules of feedback at the same time!

Robin, an aspiring political candidate, had been canvassing with his political mentor, **Peter**. Robin was young, fresh faced and very enthusiastic. Peter was a bit of an academic, able quickly to see wider political impact, with extensive knowledge of political history and had a real sense of what he knew to be right in his rule book. At the end of the day's campaigning they returned to their 'battle bus' to consider events. Peter was concerned that Robin could not really see the wood for the trees and that the key pointers for a better performance by Peter the next day were being lost.

He decided to sharpen the feedback: 'Robin, I would like you to stop being so considerate of others and agreeing with everything said; to start being more critical and analytical, conceptualizing and seeing the wider political point in what people are saying; and to continue your enthusiastic way of generating ideas for different ways of doing things and continue the way you are supporting me in my role as your adviser.'

Robin now has two specific behaviours to change for improved performance, and reassurance about two other things he is doing well and should continue. Two points are enough to take in; he will be able to see the difference at the end of the following day's programme and it focuses on the two things that Peter particularly feels will make a difference to Robin's performance.

Progress now

Imagine that you are going to give feedback using the technique Stop, Start, Continue. It goes like this:

This is what I would like you to stop doing that you are currently doing. _____

This is what I would like you to start doing that you are currently not doing. _____

These are things that you do that I want you to continue doing.

_____

Think now of someone you would like to give feedback to using this technique, and make a note of the things you would say. Now that you have done this, it will be easier to do it for real and to make a positive impact.

Here is another technique for structuring feedback.

I would be concerned if _____

I would be delighted if _____

These two simple sentences will give the person receiving the feedback the chance to focus on crucial matters.

WHAT DOES YOUR FEEDBACK SAY ABOUT YOURSELF?

When you see a worthy person, endeavour to emulate him. When you see an unworthy person, then examine your inner self.

Confucius

Notice what you notice in others, in particular the things that seem to get an exaggerated reaction from you. The things that instantly get under your skin, or the things that you find instantly appealing. What are the things that literally shout at you when you encounter someone else? Look again at the things you have just asked someone else to stop, start and continue.

These may be things that also have a meaning for you. The statement, 'it takes one to know one' works on the principle that you must have some way of recognizing something for, or from, yourself before you develop the ability to see it in others. There is so much to observe in others; what is it that we have deleted, distorted and generalized in order to come to this particular conclusion? It may be because we already recognize this pattern or behaviour trait in ourselves. This is known as mirroring.

Because you may be reluctant to acknowledge any negative traits that you dislike or fear in yourself, they most often emerge in your relationships with others. This is known as projection. You can also project what you like about yourself when noticing positive attributes in others. You project when you notice or react to some particular behaviour in another person that is really an unrecognized part of yourself.

You may know this is true when you think about how different people see different things in the same person's behaviour. How do you see what you see? It may be that you see it because you recognize it so well in yourself. What have you asked others to stop that you would like to stop in your own behaviour? What have you asked others to start that you may want to start doing more of yourself? What do you already do that you have asked others to continue?

Progress now

Thinking about the things you notice in others, metaphorically hold a mirror in front of you and, instead of their face, look at what you could notice about yourself and see how you may be projecting this. The mirror can tell you about yourself and the greatest risk in projection is often that it blurs your view of others, distorting your vision, which in turn limits your capacity to see objectively and relate more humanely. If you do not attend to the mirror, you may not distinguish the reality of the view of the other person through the confusing blur of your own unacknowledged impression of yourself.

Progress now

The purpose of this exercise is to highlight the issues that elicit a very strong response in you, and then to recognize that these may have meaning for you and say something about your own behaviours and issues. The purpose is to hold the mirror up and see your own behaviours and issues and give you some insight into yourself.

List all the qualities you do not like in others; for example greed, conceit, indecisiveness, slowness, sarcasm, rudeness etc. When the list is complete highlight those that you not only dislike, but also that you hate, loathe, abhor.

This shorter final list, consisting of four or five pet hates, is likely to be a reasonably accurate picture of your own shadow. As you look at the list you will begin to recognize the things that lurk in your shadow and know that you can face them.

The above exercise uses the principle that 'we recognize in others what we already recognize so well about ourselves'. You may loathe in others what you loathe about yourself. An easy way to remember the principle is 'perception is projection'.

THE BIG AND THE LITTLE PICTURE: GETTING THEM BOTH RIGHT

Feedback and the information that it gives will help in situations where you want to negotiate or agree an outcome. Many people go into discussions or negotiations with a strong position and then proceed either to talk at cross purposes with the other party, or play a sort of tug of war that does not seem to get anywhere until one or both parties give up with exhaustion. Wouldn't it be great to have a way of channelling energy more positively and finding ways of giving or producing things that get the response you want rather than the one you don't want.

Charles and Jacqueline run a successful partnership. Every year, their company has a big Christmas party to celebrate the year and acknowledge and appreciate each other. Jacqueline has traditionally organized this party and last year Charles felt Jacqueline was disappointed with the gift he had given her as his appreciation. This year he was determined to get it right. Jacqueline just loves presents. But she already has almost everything that Charles can think of. He asks her what she would like. Jacqueline just says, 'Oh anything, I don't mind.' Charles wants his present to be something she will use regularly and value. He cares about what he gets her and it has to be just right. So he asks her again for some suggestions or ideas. She responds with, 'I don't really mind, as long as it is lovely.' So no hints there!

As Christmas approaches, he finds himself increasingly exasperated and finally suggests three things that he thinks she would use. She says, 'Any of them would be fine.' He notes she didn't say 'brilliant' or 'fantastic' but at least he knew she thought they would be OK. He now felt he could make a decision about what present to get. He is very aware of how busy Jacqueline is, so he takes the time to let her know three or four things that he would find useful so she does not have to worry about what to give him. He is good at being thoughtful like that.

At the party, they exchange their gifts. Jacqueline said her gift was 'nice' (is that as good as 'lovely'?) and she gave Charles something that was very handsome and (he thinks) is a handcrafted paperweight, but not one of the things on the list he had helpfully given her. Charles said how 'impressive' it was and yet was a little disappointed that he had not been given one of the things on his list. So how was it that after going to so much effort, this exchange of presents still was not quite right?

How Charles could have made an appropriate choice is described below, and will help you make sure your choices — whether they are business proposals, tenders, offers of assistance, or presents for your friends — hit the right mark.

THE GIFT OF MEETING CRITERIA

There was a mismatch of criteria for a 'great' present. In Charles's world, the criteria for great presents are that something has to be really useful (and so prefers to be asked what he wants so the present is never wasted). In Jacqueline's world, the criteria for a great present is that it has to be a surprise, and it must be kept a secret so that at the moment it is opened, all the anticipation and excitement can be fully experienced. How was Charles supposed to know that?

Here is how he could have known. He could have found out Jacqueline's criteria, by using a technique called *chunking*, by going 'up' or 'down' levels of influence. Chunking up leads to higher abstractions and chunking down leads to more specific examples.

To ask questions that lead you to a higher level ask, 'What is important about that?' or 'What will that give you?' When you ask these questions you can begin to go up in steps to the other person's highest criteria or values. It is a good use of precision questioning as discussed in Chapter 8.

So Charles could have asked Jacqueline, 'What is important to you about a Christmas present?' The answer would have been, 'It is fun receiving presents.' What is important about receiving presents? 'There is a real sense of occasion about it?' What's important about that? 'It is great to be excited.' What does excitement give you? 'The shared excitement is the real "gift"! That is what I really want.'

In this example, Charles has now 'chunked up' and found out a lot about Jacqueline's criteria for a great present. There is even more valuable data available to Charles by then chunking down. To do this, the magic question is, 'What would an example of that be?' or 'What specifically?'

He could ask about 'shared excitement; what would an example of that be?' 'Everyone being together and opening presents one at a time with everyone watching and getting excited.' What would an example of getting excited be? 'When you are holding the beautifully wrapped present and imagining what might be inside it. Lots of possibilities go through my mind and the tension builds.' What specifically is the exciting bit? 'The fantastic surprise when you finally reveal the present!'

This may seem a trivial example, however the same approach is also true within organizations. This example can help you to see that different people have different expectations from the same generalized words.

When working within an organization we came across a team where team members had very different perceptions of the same leader. One member of a team was telling us how she wished her manager would trust her enough to let her get on with her work without checking up on her all of the time. Another member of the same team said that he found the way the manager asked if he was OK or if he needed any help at fairly regular intervals demonstrated how supportive the manager was.

In this case the same behaviour – asking if a person is OK or if they need any help at fairly regular intervals – impacts on different criterion for the two people, either lack of trust or supportive.

In order to influence others or to manage people successfully, you need to be sure that you are operating using 'criteria' that will satisfy their criteria rather than your own. Criteria equivalents are the little behaviours that represent the higher held beliefs and values.

An added bonus of understanding chunking is that you can greatly increase the rapport you have with people if you are talking at the same level of detail or abstraction with them. This is particularly helpful in negotiation or going for a win–win outcome.

COLLABORATIVE OUTCOMES – HOW TO WIN AT WIN–WIN

Some people's concept of negotiation is that there is one winner and one loser. Stalled negotiations or drastic compromises one the other hand can give you a lose–lose situation. In the collaborative outcome technique you are going for a win–win outcome. You can learn how to create solutions from what might originally seem implacable positions.

The following case uses the example of a holiday to illustrate the collaborative outcomes technique. It applies equally to other situations and it was the negotiation technique used between the Egyptians and the Israelis which brought about the creation of the Gaza strip which has underpinned stability between these two countries.

A regional business leader really wanted a two-week break to re-charge his batteries. The problem was that he wanted to go skiing in Colorado and his partner wanted to go to Kathmandu and then trek in Nepal. They both had their hearts set on their idea of a holiday and, having done research and imagined what it would be like, both were reluctant to let go of their dream holiday. The impasse was creating tension and he could not resolve it. We discussed the options. They could have agreed to have one week in Colorado and one week in Kathmandu but that would have been a compromise and not fully satisfying to either of them. They could have agreed on his holiday and that would have been a win–lose result (and vice versa).

The regional business leader eventually stated the end in mind was to have a great holiday. We then asked, 'What do you both want' and got the Colorado/Kathmandu difference.

What is Colorado like? We got a detailed description. What is Kathmandu like? Another description.

We then asked him what was important to him about his holiday? He said:

1 Being in a wild place.

2 Physical challenges.

3 Being pampered in the evenings.

4 Away from it all.

5 Meeting like-minded people.

The next question, 'What is important to your partner about her holiday?' resulted in this list:

1 Going somewhere very different from other holidays they had had.

2 Walking in a rarefied environment.

3 Proving to myself I can handle a harsh, stark environment.

4 Having time to talk and think away from daily pressures.

We noted some similar outcomes on their lists. We then asked them to think of at least three other solutions that could incorporate the nine outcomes on the lists. We told them that they could be as whacky or adventurous as they like. One of the made up solutions had to be at least as good as and preferably better than the original Colorado/Kathmandu they had previously set their heart on. Their agreed dream holiday was two weeks in Australia, sea kayaking, diving and trekking in the remote and beautiful coastal reefs near the Kimberley Ranges. This met all their criteria, and their obvious renewed enthusiasm for the holiday and each other was an added bonus.

You can use this same technique whenever there seem to be two intractable positions. It is particularly valuable in negotiations to resolve outward conflict.

CHAPTER 10

Balancing Leadership and Life

They who dream by day are cognisant of many things, which escape those who dream only by night.

EDGAR ALLAN POE

Working ourselves to death? The answer is no.

JOHN R. O'NEIL

THE NOTION OF BALANCE FOR PERFORMANCE

Creating balance in your life allows you to function at maximum effectiveness. When you attain this balance you are at ease with yourself, relaxed, able to give the best of yourself and, by doing so, bring out the best in others. Balance is about being well tuned – then you can drive on to achieve remarkable results.

From time to time stand back to reflect and take stock. Look at the past month and ask, 'When was I effective; when was I full of energy? When did I have time for a moment to myself?' You can also consider how the balance (or lack of it) in your life fits with how you want to be. You may be absolutely sure that everything **is** OK and that if you keep going on the current course it will be fine. You may like to ask yourself, 'Is this true for one more month? one more year? three years? five years? until our children leave home? until we retire?'

A common trait of leaders who lead with ease is a sense of having balance in and between all aspects of their life. The following case studies show helpful ways of managing balance. Each leader has their own measure of balance and feels they have it 'right'. You can examine what they have done to achieve this and then examine how you too can improve balance in your life.

David is the leader of his own precision engineering business that supplies the performance car market. He is a busy man who achieves more than most. We talked to him about his diary, as it seemed an acceptable material sign of his ability to make commitments and to manage his time. The system that lies behind his diary is unusual, although the diary itself is perfectly normal, and yet it has to be just the right one: it must be small enough to fit in his pocket; it must have a month to view; notes of appointments only get entered; no more than four (or so) things are entered in any day; Routine 'stuff' does not get listed. He uses a system of colours to highlight entries: holidays – green; very important things – pinky red; important things – orange; personal development and meeting up with personal development group of other directors – blue.

When asked what is important about his diary, he said, 'It's about being in control. I need to feel comfortable. It's good to have good time and balance management. I believe that my ideas are good ones. I used to tend to pack too much in, and now I am beginning to feel more comfortable with "space". But not too much of it, as I will soon want to be doing something again.'

At a single view, David can judge if he has the balance of his life right at any time. He is going for a balanced rainbow with clean white space on weekends. He is keen to avoid:

- Too much pink – being overstretched
- Too much orange – too much volume, not enough excitement
- No blue – out of touch with peers
- No green – need to plan to relax and do things for family and me. Weekends not clear doesn't give space for spontaneity and relaxation.

'This strategy applies to big things. I don't put daily things in my diary. I need to see clearly what the targets are.'

In her mid-thirties **Penny Hughes** became the first woman, the youngest person and the first Briton to take on the role of President of Coca-Cola Great Britain and Ireland. Having made a meteoric rise, she was determined to keep a balance between her home and her family life. She said, 'Life comes first but business is a fundamental part of life, and if there were an imbalance either way, I would correct it.' She worked reasonable hours, from 8.30 or 9.00 a.m. until 6.00 or 6.30 in the evening and never took work home or worked at the weekend. She stated, 'Those are my rules. If ever I have a job that takes more time, I'll probably pack it in. It is so important to enjoy life. In fact, I believe that it is this confidence and stability that allows you to do your job. I get up every morning and look forward to work. If I was tired, or making too many compromises, I wouldn't.'

CREATING BALANCE THROUGH RECOGNITION OF VALUES

Both these case studies show people who have addressed the need for balance in their life and have done something about it. They have identified their values and know how to achieve what they want. They understand the rewards this balance gives them. In this section, you will learn how to identify the balance in your life.

It may be that most facets of *your* life feel great and yet there may be one aspect that concerns you or does not feel quite right. It may be your weight or fitness, a relationship, or finding a way to relax. You may have a brilliant diet that helps you to stay physically and mentally in trim, or rush from convenience meal to strong cup of coffee. You may have clear lungs and a strong heartbeat, or wheeze on the stairs or have palpitations and rapid heartbeat moments.

You will know which factors are a concern for you and that you want to pay attention to the balance you have in your life. Remember, you are in control of you, and have choices about what and how you do things that will lead you to the balanced way you really want to live your life. Different people value different things in their life. There are no universal rules, no formulae, only what feels balanced to you.

Values are the things that you hold important to yourself. They are what tell you when you are in or out of alignment. David values achieving his goals in a way that leaves him with energy to face the next challenge. He values holidays, personal development and time with his family to do things 'on a whim'. Penny Hughes also values achievement, motherhood, family life and clear boundaries. She invests in her own health as she values her health and well-being. Your values are how you calibrate happiness or contentment.

Once you have identified your values, you will sift, delete, distort and generalize in their honour! Many people hold some values in common. These common values are what determine the norms of the society you live in.

The development of values

Values are developed as we grow up. Our first seven years are characterized by 'imprinting'. This is the stage in our life where others can easily imprint on us values that they hold, and we are most likely not to question but to adopt them wholeheartedly.

Development from ages 13 to 18 can be typified as 'experiment'. This is when you test if the values fed to you, hold for you. This is when you push to find the boundaries, your time of changing loyalties.

In adulthood, you refine your values. When you work, own things and have standards that manifest themselves in all sorts of idiosyncratic ways such as clothes, labels, membership of groups, then you know you have begun to lay out your initial set of values against which you judge whether things are important to you or not.

Whole of life values

To put the world in order, we must first put the nation in order; to put the nation in order, we must first put the family in order; to put the family in order, we must first cultivate our personal life; we must first set our hearts right.

Confucius

You may find that you have different values for different sectors of your life. You may find that you also have some that are true in all contexts and these are likely to be elevated to beliefs. The following technique provides a way to check firstly the balance you want between different sectors and secondly the particular values in each sector.

Life pie

Imagine your life to be like a pie that has different sized slices. Typically the pie might be divided into the following segments:

Work/career	Spirituality and personal development
Family	Friends/community/relationship
Health and hygiene	Travel/holidays/adventures
Leisure	Eating and socializing
Home or security	

You will notice that money is not on this list. Money is most often a 'means value' rather than an 'ends value'. If you ask, 'What is important about money?' or 'What does that give us?' you may find that it is security, or freedom to choose. It is a means to the more valued end.

We recently coached a leader from a leading edge pharmaceuticals company to an understanding of her values.

Current balance We asked **Simone** to draw her own values pie with her own labels for each slice and to divide the size of each slice according to the time she invested in each segment.

Desired balance Simone was then asked to think about how she would like to invest her time in the future to balance her life as a leader according to what *she* really wanted rather than what she thought others might expect of her.

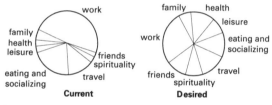

Current   **Desired**

Questions to support change Simone was surprised that she was already beginning to imagine the sorts of changes she could see herself making in order to adjust the balance. By asking the question, 'What would it take to achieve that shift?' she was able to formulate a plan. When considering some of the shifts, a question that was helpful to remove a block in her mind was 'What stops you from making that change?' or 'What is it you get from the current situation that rewards you – and how else could you have a better reward in your new, balanced life?'

(229)

At the end of the coaching sessions with Simone, she had a clearer picture of her desired life balance by looking at her desired 'life pie'. She had begun to see things as she wanted them as opposed to just dwelling on how things were not right.

Progress now

Mapping out your desired balance

Now that you have seen the process that Simone went through you have the tools to do this for yourself.

1   Draw a circle and map out your own life segments according to how you are **currently** investing your time and energies. Be honest with yourself.

2   Map out the desired balance you want in your life. Make this what you want as opposed to what you think other people may want.

3   Ask yourself the questions that support change, 'What would it take to achieve this change?', 'What stops me from changing?', 'What gains and rewards do I get in the current balance – and how could I have better rewards in the new, more desirable, balance?'

4   What would be your first step to starting this re-balancing exercise? What little, or big, changes could you make that will get the momentum for desirable change started?

Values within a slice of life

Having mapped out the broad balance you would prefer, how do you know if you have got what you need within each slice? Take work for example. How do you know if you are in the right kind of work? You can help answer that question by understanding the component elements that you really value in each slice of your life. What are 'elements' that, if they are in your working life in the right quantities, give you that satisfying feeling of harmony and stability?

Eliciting values

We worked with Simone to go through an exercise to elicit her values for work. Simone chose to call it career. We began by working through a process that helped her identify what would really be important to her for 'career' to be really good. Later you will have the opportunity to use these same questions to elicit your values.

Label the slice

'In describing this slice of your life, what would you call that?' (Work, career, occupation, profession, livelihood etc.)

Simone's response was an emphatic use of the word 'career'. It was important to use her own word as the label for this slice of her life pie.

Generate your list of values for this slice

What would be important to you, Simone, for a career to be really good?

'Part of a healthy wider system – it has to be congruent.'

What else has to be there for career to be great?

'I need to feel connected.'

What else?

'Working on new experiences – variety.'

What else needs to be there for you?

'Good relationships at work – ones that grow.'

When you've got all of those, what else needs to be there?

'Self esteem and belief that I can do it' and 'Others recognize my contribution.' She then refined her statement to 'Making a valued contribution.'

Check for anything missing

'If you've got all those is there anything else that would cause you to leave?'

Simone answered '*Enjoyment*' and this was added to list. (There may or may not have been anything to add at this stage.)

Simone now had a list of seven items which she condensed into the following words. These represent her work values and are indicators to know if her current or next job is in line with what she wants.

A   Healthy wider system

B   Connected

C   Variety

D   Developing good relationships

E   High self belief and esteem

F   Recognition

G   Enjoyment

The value of the right order

This list is even more useful when the values are in order. This is because you may be lucky enough to find a career that satisfies everything you want, and you may not. If it does not, having the items at the top of the list rather than the bottom will be important. We went through these questions with Simone for getting her 'career' values in the right order.

'Of all of these, Simone, if you could have only one, which would it be?'

'High self belief and esteem.'

'Is high self belief and esteem more important than A? Is high self belief and esteem more important than B?, Is high self belief and esteem more important than C?' etc. (If something else was more important than high self belief and esteem move it to the top of the list and go through the process again). High self belief and esteem now becomes A at the top of the list.

We then asked Simone to choose the value that she thought was next important. Simone chose D. 'Is D (developing good relationships) more important than C?' etc. This was done until we had checked each item. At any point where Simone felt unsure, we asked the question, 'If you could have only one of these, which would it be?' That choice should then be the higher one on the list.

Check by choice

To complete this technique of eliciting a list of values and getting them in the right order, it is useful to cross check. We did this by saying, 'I am going to offer you a choice of jobs. One is with a company that has a clear and honourable purpose and a healthy working culture where you will be encouraged to connect with your ideas and build strong relationships with those you work with (A, B and C on her list). The other is a job where you will enjoy what you are doing and get recognition (F and G). If you can have one job, and not the other, which would you choose?' If the order in the list were correct for Simone, she would choose the first job offered; if she chose the second job, it might be that the order was not right and that enjoyment and recognition should be higher on her list. In this case, Simone chose the first job.

This list was then of great value to Simone as a yardstick for knowing whether what she was currently doing was a good match to her values. It helped her to see what she needed more of or less of in her current career position and was even more valuable in allowing her to test options in a reorganization that took place soon after in her company.

Checking the list in each segment

Over a couple of sessions, Simone worked through what values she held in each segment of her life pie. This simple process helped Simone bring focus and balance back into her life and to begin to structure her time and energies to coincide with what was of value to her. And when you get that right, work or career, even when it remains busy, becomes somehow 'lighter' and you achieve a sense of balance and harmony in your life.

Progress now

This technique allows you to see the values you ascribe to any segment of your life. The same approach could then be taken for any or all of the segments in your life pie, if you wished to do that.

You may wish to ask someone else to pose the questions in this exercise and record the answers for you, so that you can let your mind attend to generating the responses. If you do this exercise on your own, let your intuitive answers come out, as it is your unconscious that can hold the key to this being a revealing and rewarding insight into yourself.

Here are the questions for the technique of eliciting values.

1 Name the segment of the life pie you are talking about. (x)
2 What is important to you about (x)?
3 What has to be there for (x) to be great?
4 What else?
5 What else needs to be there for you to know (x) is really good?
6 When you have all those, what else needs to be there?

When you feel you have your list, check with this question:

7 If you had all those is there anything else that would cause you to leave? Now put these values for this slice of your life pie into an order. Begin with the question:

8 If you could have only one of these things on the list, which would it be?

9 Now cross check. Is A more important than B, more important than C etc. until you have been through the list. At any point if something else is more important go back to the beginning of step 9, cross checking the new order.

10 You now have the value that is at the top of the list. The next stage is to list what is the next most important thing and cross check this in the same way as 9 until you have all your values for this segment of your pie in order.

11 Finally, get someone to invent two jobs. The first will have a mixture of the top half of the list of values, and the second job offer will have a mixture of the lower half. If you choose the first job, it is likely that your list is accurate; if you don't, you may want to re-visit the process above to rework your order.

You can repeat this process for some or every segment of your pie and see where you are getting what you value, and where you are not. This gives you the choice to change what you are doing now so you can get more of what is important to you.

SHINY SIDES AND DULL SIDES

Most of our behaviours have a shiny side and sometimes also a dull side; an attribute can also be a weakness. For example, enthusiasm can also be seen as overbearing. Reflection can also be seen as withdrawal.

 When I meet people who have had a great triumph, I tell them that I hope it doesn't hurt them too much.

Carl Gustav Jung

You have spent time already in this chapter seeing ways to create the life balance you want and you have looked at the values within slices of your life. This gives you a clear picture of how you want your life to be. And yet there may be things that have not been addressed. Things that lurk at the back of your mind or perhaps that you deny publicly – a shadow that follows your success in leading.

The concept of a shadow appears in two forms – the 'dull' side to your otherwise shining attributes and the more deeply seated shadows that may exist in your life. The first concept is simply that our approach to some things may not have the impact we intend. We may tip things out of kilter by overdoing or underdoing the way we do them. We will explore this through a case study. The second, the shadow, is the dark, vaguely shaped companion that is inseparable from our shape. It can be difficult to pin down and it has a slightly ominous feel about it. If a shadow grows too dark and large, nothing can thrive in its shade. In psychology, the shadow has a more precise set of meanings and can be a useful tool for understanding how the greatest and brightest leaders can falter.

The dull side of the coin

Your character can appear flawed when the impact of an attribute becomes more (or less) than what is needed. You can appear 'out of kilter' when good aspects of your character have been overstretched or concentrated to the point where they tip the balance of the high performance vehicle you wish to be and you begin to misfire. The shiny side of the coin can begin to be seen as dull.

Manoj was a bright leader of a team that ran a busy retail clothing outlet. He had always wanted to lead his team to become the top performing store and he had achieved it with them topping the league ladder. Manoj had now been offered a promotion to a better, bigger, newer store based on his performance. When asked what were the characteristics about him that had helped him to achieve his success, he replied, 'I am confident in my actions, and not afraid to take big decisions. I have made a big commitment to this job. I am pretty dedicated and the success of the store means a lot to me. I am able to charm and interact well with customers and I have a sense of humour and wit that helps me get along with people. I have clear and high standards and I control everything to ensure that targets are met. In particular, I watch the pennies so we don't go over budget.'

That all sounded good, and yet I needed to ask Manoj some questions to understand how things were below the surface. 'Do you think your team are happy?' and 'Are you really happy?' 'No' and 'No' were his responses.

As a successful leader, you may struggle in appropriate use of power, relationships, responsibilities, and your own well-being. Or you may not. It is critical to recognize that less desirable aspects of your behaviours may be showing your endeavours in a dull light. It may be that you already have evidence of this whether it be a stress-related condition, tension at work, unhappy relationship, need for adrenalin rushes to keep you going or overwhelming fatigue. It may be clear and recognizable or just a whisper that disturbs you. Some of these descriptions may be recognizable in yourself or others.

Manoj aimed to talk to his staff about how they saw his characteristics as a leader so that he could learn from their feedback and make adjustments before he moved to the next step in his career. They did recognize his positive traits and valued them; however, they also saw them in a more extreme form on a regular basis. One of his section heads said to me, 'Manoj would be even better than he is now if he just toned himself down a bit and trusted us to do things for ourselves. He never considers that he might be wrong, and yet he exhausts himself checking up on us all the time. He is too busy to say we are doing a good job, except when we have to stay after work for one of his team events. I have got loads of ideas that could make us even better than best, but I don't say them any more after the last time he made a wise crack when I tried to describe what I had in mind. He says he is committed, but that just means he follows company procedures and policies without regard to the impact on us. He can be ruthless.'

The results of the feedback showed Manoj that he was in danger of drifting to the dull side of his desirable attributes. These showed themselves as follows.

Shining form	Dull form
Commitment	Blind faith
Confidence	Infallibility
Witty	Abrasive
Brave	Foolhardy
Control	Inflexible
Charm	Manipulation
Economic	False economy
Dedicated	Workaholic

Progress now

List your own desirable or shining character traits and identify what that would look like if it took on a dull form.

Shining form	Dull form

Confronting the darker shadows

We are as great as our finest idea and as weak as our smallest obsession.

The recognizing and acknowledgement of fear is a mark of wisdom. I call it my black dog.

Winston Churchill

We have recognized the dull form of attributes. And beyond this there may be this other form of presence or shadow. At times the shadow may be so well hidden that we do not recognize its existence. You may hide issues well in your shadows and deprive them of light, even deny their presence at all, and yet know they are there. A hidden secret, a denied occurrence, a lie, an action that was cowardly, or a cover up. The things you hope no one will ever find out about.

Shadows affect us as individuals

You know these darker elements are there, and yet have relegated them from your conscious thoughts.

Every life is affected by the shadow to some extent, and it is useful to look at what happens to high achievers who do not attend to their shadow — leaders in business at Enron falsifying accounts; in sport, Hanse Cronje taking bribes and Mike Tyson's violent behaviour; in politics, Bill Clinton's relationships with women, Richard Nixon's lying, and Robert Mugabe of Zimbabwe's intimidation of opposition politicians and media. These are all examples overshadowing their lives, and you will know of examples in your own worlds too. Leaders are constantly told they should show no weaknesses, admit no mistakes, and show no impropriety: be saints, if possible. And then their mythical success explodes across the front pages.

Family or group shadows

As a family or a group you can also have shadows, secrets and names that must not be mentioned. There are organizational and corporate shadows too. The family shadow may contain secrets, denied emotions, or hidden behaviours that affect the dynamics. There may be collusion to cover up violence, alcohol or drug use or other corruption. High profile families, especially those with the trappings of mythical success, may carry a heavy shadow. At organizational level, there may exist the shadow of corruption, institutional racism or sexism. On the world stage, this typically results in groups being divided into enemies or scapegoats and the Third Reich, the Cold War, and ethnic cleansing are all manifestations of collective shadow.

Light onto the shadow

Why, then, is it important to address the shadow in your life? Looking back at the idea of the values pie, you can recognize that the way you feel about life when your energies are being invested in the way you want them to be is very different from how you feel when they are not. When you have the alignment right, you may well feel energy from what you are doing, rather than feeling drained.

You can experience the same boost in your energy and self esteem when you face and address the matters that lurk in your shadows. You may remember from childhood, or more recently, how it feels to track a lie you have told. The energy it took to remember the untruth would be considerable and may have been better spent doing something braver and truthful.

 When you stand back and face your issues, a glimpse of light falls on the face in the shadow.

Rabbi Lionel Blue

Progress now

This brief questionnaire will give you a tool to recognize shadows for yourself and to shine some light on them.

1 Is your diary saturated with 'important' dates? ☐ ☐
Yes No

2 Do you find less and less time for family and friends? ☐ ☐
Yes No

3 Do you spend little time alone, in fact avoid it? ☐ ☐
Yes No

4 Have you given up some small ritual that refreshed you, like a walk or a quiet cup of tea on the porch? ☐ ☐
Yes No

5 Is competition your primary mode of interacting with others? ☐ ☐
Yes No

6 Is winning central to your sense of self-worth? ☐ ☐
Yes No

7 Are your competitor's losses even more satisfying than your own gains? ☐ ☐
Yes No

8 When your team accomplishes something, do you fret about your share not being large enough or your credit too small? ☐ ☐
Yes No

9 Is your world divided into winners and losers? ☐ ☐
Yes No

10	Have the trappings and symbols of power become crucial to your self-definition?	☐ Yes ☐ No
11	Do you feel upset if people get your title wrong or fail to recognize you?	☐ Yes ☐ No
12	Are you buying things to fit or bolster your image?	☐ Yes ☐ No
13	Are your trophies shielding feelings of inadequacy?	☐ Yes ☐ No
14	Do you overextend or abuse your natural talents?	☐ Yes ☐ No
15	For example, if you are good at relating to people and getting them to confide in you, do you end up misusing their trust?	☐ Yes ☐ No
16	Or do you use your skill with numbers, words, memory, or whatever to show off, dominate or humiliate others?	☐ Yes ☐ No
17	Do you neglect developing your latent gifts because you can always count on the old tricks?	☐ Yes ☐ No
18	When you find yourself stuck, unable to resolve difficulties in your career or relationships, do you invent all sorts of external reasons – bad luck, the economy, other people's weakness or ineptitude – to explain your problem?	☐ Yes ☐ No
19	Do you invariably find your associates or employees flawed and unreliable?	☐ Yes ☐ No

20	When you get bad news or criticism, do you brood on it or take more than your just share of blame for it?	☐ ☐ Yes No
21	Do you dwell on critical remarks or slights, imagining what you could have done to avoid them?	☐ ☐ Yes No
22	Do you overlook and downplay compliments or feel unworthy of them?	☐ ☐ Yes No
23	Has the need for control and the exercise of power become a desperate and depleting game?	☐ ☐ Yes No
24	Do small irritants and vexing details bother you out of proportion?	☐ ☐ Yes No
25	Are you less tolerant of delays, change in schedules, slow service?	☐ ☐ Yes No
26	Are you sometimes flooded with negative emotions that surprise you by their intensity, cripple your effectiveness, and alienate those around you?	☐ ☐ Yes No
27	Does anger boil into rage over trivial events like a car cutting you off or someone pushing ahead of you in line?	☐ ☐ Yes No
28	Have you become rigid in your views and the way you take in information, in what you consider valuable or acceptable?	☐ ☐ Yes No
29	Are you so committed to what demands attention right now that you can't plan for the future?	☐ ☐ Yes No
30	Are opportunities for change passing you by because you can't see them or can't change gears?	☐ ☐ Yes No

Analysing your shadow

The questionnaire has given you some notion of a shadow's symptoms. Check against the sections below how many yeses you scored. If you have predominantly scored yes, this may be an area of concern for you.

Q 1–4 – The Whirl of Commitments

Do you look at your own diary and see it filled? If you do, remember you approved each appointment and you must want it that way. Being in demand is a basic need to be significant. But if you feel uncomfortable alone with yourself, it may mean that you have concerns about who you are and what you are doing.

Q 5–9 – The Spur of Competition

A predominance of yes answers in this section means you live in a competitive world where you compete out of habit. You may always need to be on top and you may be concerned about other people's accomplishments. In this area you may be engaged and end up exhausted by a perpetual fight with yourself.

Q 10–13 – Lack of Self Esteem

High scores of yes in this set point to a potential lack of self esteem and the risk of a fragile ego. You may require external material symbols, such as a large office, to support you.

Q 14–17 – Over-extended Talents

In this set you may have a natural talent, such as a quick mind and sharp tongue. As you become more involved you may find that your comments, quick in reply, may become more ascerbic and turn your colleagues against you.

Q 18–19 – It's Their Fault

Yes in this set means you ascribe success to yourself and failure to others. You can blind yourself to your own failings. It's as if the magic that made you successful will vanish if you admit failure.

Q 20–22 – I'm Lucky to be Successful

When others compliment you on a good job you can't connect to their sincerity. You feel a fraud about your success. You can take on too much blame. Your inner critic becomes dominant.

Q 23–25 – The Need for Power and Control

If you need to control issues, unacceptable feelings of powerlessness become your shadow. Habits that served you well in the past, such as attention to detail, may become obsessions that impact on everyone.

Q 26–27 – Free-floating Anger

Yes in these areas means you are angry and the anger may reflect deeply buried emotional needs that require attention. If there is this form of anger, your shadow is calling for attention.

Q 28–30 – Rigidity of Views

You may tend to stick with what works but to succeed in the long term you need to be flexible and adaptive. As you grow older there is a chance of you becoming more rigid. Do you argue for the prevailing wisdom when someone less powerful argues for a change?

CHAPTER 11

Now Go and BE Your Best

Get action. Seize the moment. Man was never intended to become an oyster.

THEODORE ROOSEVELT

He did what he did in spite of his fear. No man can be braver than that.

WINSTON CHURCHILL SPEAKING OF A PREWAR SUPPORTER AS PORTRAYED IN A BBC TELEVISION PROGRAMME

GETTING YOU READY

In this book you have had the opportunity to address things in your world that you wish to influence. You have been taken through techniques and exercises that give you the tools to address and deal with those things that really matter to you. You now have real choice about what you do in developing your leadership.

Many of you will not need the remaining three techniques that are included in this chapter, and yet for others they will be the most important pages in the whole book.

You may ponder on the state of mind you would like to be in to address issues from your past and get yourself ready for your future. Use the techniques of resourceful states and anchoring to help you get ready to make some powerful changes.

FEAR FROM THE PAST

It is natural to have fears and often they become part of our make up. These fears do not have to be morbid or extreme. If you do have fears on this scale, they are phobias and we will deal with those later in this chapter.

Many people have more general fears that hold them back. It may be a fear of speaking in front of a group, or a fear of writing their ideas down. It could be a fear of interviews or a reluctance to take responsibility.

The experiences that contributed to you holding this belief or fear first happened at a time in your life when you did not have all the resources you needed to deal with it. Subsequently, whenever you then experienced or anticipated this thing, you also experienced it as fearful. Now every time you encounter a similar situation you put the label of fear on it. Being fearful reinforces the fear and just adds to the whole unhelpful cycle you have set up. You will now be given a technique that will help you to address those fears, giving you the choice to change.

Timelines

Creating a timeline to walk along is a helpful technique for exploring time and feelings and experiences associated with those times. The first stage of timeline work is to identify where you experience your past. It can be good fun to just close your eyes and point in the direction you think represents your past. Do the same for the direction of your future. You will be amazed at the different ways different people can experience this.

For these timeline exercises, we will also be asking you to identify a line on the ground, establishing which direction is past and which is future and where on the line, the present is. To use the timeline you will also be using the techniques of perceptual positions and association and dissociation (Chapter 6).

Many of us have experiences from the past that have a lasting impact. It is possible for an experience to subconsciously inhibit us in subsequent years. Examples may be where we say, 'Well, I never have been able to do . . .' or 'When faced with . . . I always . . .' These are known as *limiting beliefs*. Timelines can help by reframing experiences that initiated the original belief.

Graham was tired of being 'boring but dependable' and always being the one that took matters seriously. We wanted more motivation, lightness and fun for him and his team.

We used the timeline technique to assist him to achieve this change. He imagined a line on the floor and asked him to step onto the point that represented the present. Each time he stepped on the line he was to be in 'first position' and be associated. Each time he stepped off the line he would be dissociated and in third position.

Graham was asked to step down his timeline and to pause at four or five significant occasions where he had the same feeling of being 'boring but dependable' and at each one to re-experience what it was like, what he could see, hear and feel. He recalled:

◊ Getting ready for the last AGM

◊ Completing last year's comprehensive review

◊ Preparing for his finals at University

◊ Being on the School Council

◊ Collecting his siblings from school and giving them their tea each night.

We then asked if there was an earlier experience that had the same feel about it and he added:

◊ Looking after brother at home when mother was very ill and father working away.

He had associated back into each of these experiences. He then stepped off the line and dissociated himself from those feelings. We walked him off the line and back adjacent to 'present' and asked him as the adult Graham what gift, knowledge or resource would you like to give Graham back there as a child. The resource he needed was the courage to ask for help. Graham then sent this resource to the younger self. We walked back beside the line to the time of the younger self where he stepped back onto the line and accepted this resource to ask for help. With this he could be supported and have time to enjoy himself.

259

We asked Graham to walk back on the line through each of the five times and re-experience each one with his resource in play. As he did this he was more relaxed and felt each experience as being very different with this new resource and knowledge available to him.

Finally Graham was asked to face the future and imagine the next time he would face a similar situation and step into that time with all his new resources and new history in play. As he did so he experienced his future as being fairer and more fun and far more motivating.

This technique helps people to re-print over a limiting belief (I am boring but dependable) with an enabling new belief (I can ask for support and have fun).

MANAGING A PHOBIA

There are some limiting beliefs that are so powerful that the idea of directly reliving or re-associating into them is not recommended lightly. And yet because the brain has set up in some way this intense fear or reaction it can also set it in a different way that is more enabling.

The following technique can be used with all sorts of people. It is known as 'fast phobia cure' and it does what the label says. It works with the metaphor of going to the movies.

This technique was used to coach a group by demonstrating how you could tone down an irrational and debilitating fear. In the demonstration case it was someone who was phobic about being alone in the dark. You can imagine how limiting that was for the person involved. By the end of the session, while the person may not have been completely at ease in the dark on her own, she was nevertheless able to imagine herself managing in most situations and this alone had allowed her to make choices she otherwise would have avoided.

Progress now

This is how clients have been guided through dealing with a problem.

1. Establish a resource anchor. This is just to use should your 'client' want to break state from the process at any point. Establish what fear/phobia they would like to change.

2. Acknowledge to the client the mind's ability of one-trial learning, and how the brain has learnt from one occasion always to have this reaction.

3. Imagine a blank movie screen. Ask the client to come into the theatre, sit down in the dissociated third position and see a still frame black and white image of their younger self on the screen at a time just before the onset of the bad memory. They see a time when they felt safe and secure.

4. Next, ask the client to dissociate once more from their body and come to a projection booth. As they enter the projection booth the client can now see themselves in the auditorium, looking at a black and white picture of their younger self.

5. Tell client they are going to run the black and white movie all the way through until they reach a time after the event when they know they were safe and secure. The client watches themselves watching the movie and experiences a double dissociation from the memory.

6. Ask the client to freeze-frame at the time after the event when they were safe and secure again. Now ask them to blank the screen.

7   Ask the client to run the movie backwards, in colour, at speed. Do it really fast in a few seconds. It will be like a silly cartoon, until they get back to the safe point before it started. Anchor this process with a sound.

8   Repeat the process three to five times, always starting at the blank screen and only ever running the film backwards. At this point you have a choice about whether you invite them to come back into the theatre and experience the backwards film from a single dissociated experience and then once comfortable to go into the picture itself as an associated experience. Always backwards, at speed. Use the same sound anchor.

9   Test and future pace. Ask them to imagine going into a similar situation again, and calibrate their response. If they are still experiencing a disabling reaction, go back and repeat the process until their kinesthetic reaction disappears or is manageable.

Following this group coaching session, the participants coached each other through the technique. There was a very interesting case of a woman who had an irrational fear of horses. It meant she could not relax when in country lanes, was uneasy if police or ceremonial horses were present and absolutely would turn down hospitality opportunities such as the races, polo and ceremonial occasions. It did not help her in her role, which included representing her company in a Public Relations capacity.

She was coached through the fast phobia cure technique and was also able to visualize herself coping, if not loving, future occasions where horses might be evident.

MOVING ON – MAKING CHOICES

Three wise steps

A leader once said moving on and doing things comes down to three factors.

- 🔃 Knowing what you want to do
- 🔃 Knowing how to do it
- 🔃 Creating the chance to do it.

These are three factors in creating the things you want to achieve. You might want to consider the well-formed outcome that you had the chance to formulate in Chapter 3, which will have clarified for you exactly what you want to do. If it does not yet feel compelling then your well-formed outcome may benefit from a revisit to fine-tune it a little bit more. The 'knowing how to' bit does not mean that you have to have pre-plotted every step – that is likely to be a waste of your resources. However, you may be aware of the behaviours and skills you need to have in place, but more importantly the beliefs that will support you doing all the things you have to do to achieve your outcome. And then you must take on the identity of yourself as a person that is already achieving these things.

You will need to create the 'chance to DO' the things you want to achieve. Don't hear yourself saying in a year or two, 'I always wanted to achieve . . . But I somehow never got the chance to.' Take control, make it happen and give yourself the chance to be the leader you can be for the cause you dream of.

TIME TO CHOOSE
Forward timelines

This technique is a culmination of much that you have learned in this book and will bring your future choices clearly into view and enable you to make the decision that will be right for you in achieving a significant outcome that you want.

In working through this technique you will be using the skills of outcome thinking, resourceful states, anchoring, and enabling beliefs. You will consider the leadership styles that are needed at different stages and you will really experience the 'you' that you need to be to achieve the things that you really want to achieve.

Anna was unsure of what to do next in her life. She felt she was treading water. She had generated some logical avenues for the future but could not choose or make any progress towards any of them.

She wanted to have a compelling option that she would be motivated to achieve. In Anna's case we went for a walk to a park. Anna described her three ideas for the future. We asked her to identify three different places in the park that would represent each of these futures. We then visited each one and asked her to fully associate into that future by stepping into it and imagining what it would be like. This she did and generated for each new insights and understandings of what it would really be like.

We came back to our starting point that represented her 'now'. Anna was asked to choose to step towards the future that felt the most compelling. She was now absolutely clear about which one she wanted. She went to that place and fully experienced it again. She felt great. The final part was to come back to now and recognize the steps she would have to take to achieve this outcome, identify any barriers together with the resources she would need to overcome them and step through each of these to achieve her outcome.

Anna has now made a career change and credits the future timeline technique with giving her the belief that she could do it.

Progress now

Here is the technique for forward timelines for your own use, or to coach someone else through this remarkable process.

1   Generate three or four outcomes/options for the future.

2   Find an open space or large room and identify a spot for now, and a location that represents each option.

3   Step into 'now' and associate with how things are at present.

4   Step off 'now' and begin to describe one of your options from a dissociated perspective.

5   Decide which landmark represents this option and walk to this place and identify an exact spot that will represent this option being achieved.

6   Step into this spot and fully associate with the experience of this option being achieved and being really good. Take time to get the full experience.

7   Step off the spot, break state and walk back to the 'now'.

8   Repeat steps 5 to 7 for each option.

9   Step back into 'now' and choose which option is the most compelling or feels best and walk towards it. Step into it when you reach its spot and experience it again.

10. Walk back to 'now' and designate a timeline between 'now' and the location of desired outcome.

11. Step onto the line at 'now' and begin to walk on the timeline towards your outcome until a barrier/issue is perceived. Identify the internal resources you would need to get you through this barrier. Step to the right of the line and recall a time when you had this resource and associate into that resourceful experience. Step back onto the line *with* resources and describe actions to be taken. Record these actions and resources.

12. Continue to step forward along the timeline to identify barriers, resources and actions (at each barrier repeat step 11). Record each barrier until outcome is reached and again step into it and experience it fully.

13. Now step out of that experience and walk back parallel to the timeline and repeat steps 11 and 12 using notes as a prompt. Do this as often as you want, a minimum of three to five times.

14. Homework. You should now write up the journey, barriers, resources and actions in your own words. When this is done, write up the first actions to be taken in detail and have a very clear plan of what you want to do, how you are going to do it and how to get the chance to do it.

Enjoy the motivation and momentum that flows.

GO AND DO WHAT YOU WANT TO DO

Throughout this book you have discovered ways of achieving what you want for yourself, for your cause and you have explored ways as a leader that you can achieve amazing results. You have your well-formed outcome from Chapter 3 together with the resources and techniques to make this really compelling. You can increase your effectiveness by layering all the insights, techniques and the personal learning and discovery you have had on top of your well-formed outcome to make it invincible if that is what you want. So . . . go to it . . . and enjoy your journey!

NOTES

NOTES

NOTES

NOTES